Roberto's
New
Vegan
Cooking

ALSO BY ROBERTO MARTIN

Vegan Cooking for Carnivores: Over 125 Recipes So Tasty You Won't Miss the Meat

Roberto's
New
Vegan
Cooking

125

Easy, Delicious,
REAL FOOD
RECIPES

ROBERTO
MARTIN

Da Capo
LIFE
LONG

A Member of the Perseus Books Group

Editorial production by Marrathon Production Services. www.marrathon.net

Book Design by Megan Jones Design. www.meganjonesdesign.com
Set in 10 point Bodoni Egyptian Pro

Cataloging-in-Publication data for this book is available from the Library of Congress.

First Da Capo Press edition 2015

ISBN: 978-0-7382-1732-1 (hardcover)

ISBN: 978-0-7382-1733-8 (e-book)

Published by Da Capo Press
A Member of the Perseus Books Group
www.dacapopress.com

Da Capo Press books are available at special discounts for bulk purchases in the U.S. by
corporations, institutions, and other organizations. For more information, please contact
the Special Markets Department at the Perseus Books Group, 2300 Chestnut Street,
Suite 200, Philadelphia, PA, 19103, or call (800) 810-4145, ext. 5000, or e-mail special.
markets@perseusbooks.com.

10 9 8 7 6 5 4 3 2 1

TO MY MOM

Thank you for the advice, humorous banter, and serious
talks that always took place in the kitchen.
¡Te quiero un chingo!

CONTENTS

1 DIY BASICS, STAPLES, AND SAUCES THAT WILL CHANGE YOUR LIFE (or at least your kitchen)

2 GET YOUR MORNING ON: SMOOTHIES AND OTHER BREAKFAST GOODNESS

3 MAKE YOUR LUNCH BREAK

4 I'VE GOT BIG BOWLS

5 | TREAT YOUR GREENS RIGHT

6 | A LITTLE SUMTHIN-SUMTHIN ON THE SIDE

7 | THE MAIN EVENT

8 | IF ALL GOOD MEALS MUST COME TO AN END . . . (let's go out this way)

INTRODUCTION

It was about 11:30 p.m. on a balmy summer evening when I left The Little Owl in Greenwich Village. I was tired and my face felt oily and in need a good scrubbing, but I was filled with excitement, gratitude, and the overwhelming feeling of pride. I had just cooked a dinner for about forty strangers: celebs, athletes, and various reps from media outlets. The dinner was hosted by Gardein, and they invited me to New York City to guest chef the event. The chefs who were hired to help were hard working, and although we had just met the day before, their performance was flawless. The food looked amazing and absolutely everyone was happy with the way the evening unfolded. The sensation of a meal gone right and the pride that comes with it is what I hope everyone who cooks a recipe from this book gets to feel. It makes no difference if you are cooking for a huge party, your family, your friends, or yourself, it's an endeavor that deserves attention and high-quality ingredients. We should cook with a sense of gratitude that we are not without food, and when all our efforts go well we should celebrate. I want you to feel that sense of accomplishment, and I hope this book helps.

I've been a professional chef for fifteen years, and throughout that time many sayings and mantras have come and gone, but the one that never seems to go away is "keep it simple." I must say this ten times a day. When I cook at home for my wife and kids it's usually some form of a veggie burrito or stir-fry with a side of broccoli or green beans that have been cooked with salt, pepper, and olive oil with a squeeze of lemon juice. It's just so easy and they love it.

With that in mind, what works for me with my own family, I have put a great deal of effort into making these recipes as straightforward and user-friendly as possible. When I first started creating vegan dishes, I used a lot of meat substitutes. And don't get me wrong—those are great, especially when you're in a pinch. What I consider now when I'm making a meal is cooking real food with as little manipulation as possible. I have moved away from meals based on "processed" meat substitutes in an attempt for these recipes to be the next step on your vegan journey. That feeling of pride and sensation of a meal done right? I have the same feeling when I hear from people about how they cooked something from my book and the whole family loved it. I feel blessed beyond words to be in this unique situation to be able to positively affect the lives of people I've never met, and I hope these recipes are accompanied by good times. My passion for cooking grows stronger every day and I want you to be a part of it.

Do you love being in the kitchen but sometimes you just can't do it—you've just got too much to do, and you just want to EAT? Not fast food, but REAL food? The first chapter gives you a foundation with a whole bunch of easy homemade staples; armed with these basics there is no limit to what you can throw together.

A lot of these basic DIY staples will help if you're strapped for time and still want to have a healthy meal. With these basics on hand, you can use bagged salad (add Almond Bacon

Bits, page 12, and Miso Dressing, page 53, and you've got fresh greens and dressing you'll be licking from the bowl) or a commercial veggie burger (homemade mayo, ketchup, and pickles anyone?) if you need to. These basics add a healthy element even when you have to resort to a more packaged food to get a meal on the table. With these staples on hand the transition to simple, fresh foods becomes easier. Many of these staples are also foundations for other recipes in the book. I created a range—from seriously amazing croissants to low-carb tacos to mushroom black bean burgers that the biggest 'shroom hater will devour (seriously—ask my son). There are some great dishes for when you have more time, too: daikon scallops are off the hook, and you'll never look at a blanquette the same way again. And of course dessert! Enough said.

Vegan food keeps growing in popularity—it's no longer cool, trendy, or a fad. I see more phenomenal chefs adding vegan dishes to their menus because not only is it a common request, but they have embraced how much fun and creative vegan cooking can be. I've seen a big switch in people's acceptance and willingness to explore and experience vegan food—in fact, I think it's become a new choice of cuisine for folks ("Honey, what do you want for dinner tonight? Italian? Burgers? Sushi? Vegan?"). We are making healthier and more informed decisions in terms of what we eat, and I am sure that trend will continue to grow. I hope you enjoy making these dishes as much as I enjoyed coming up with them—and as much as my family enjoys eating them.

OUTFIT YOUR KIT(CHEN): INGREDIENTS *and* TOOLS

INGREDIENTS

For the most part, the ingredients I use follow my "keep it simple" motto; you'll find these in your regular grocery store or in bulk online. Here's a list of the general ingredients I use in these recipes, with notes on anything that may seem new or unusual.

VEGGIES TO KEEP ON HAND

Beets

Broccoli

Cabbage

Carrots

Celeriac (Sometimes called "celery root," this knobby root veg is underappreciated and often overlooked. If you're not familiar with this bad boy, take a chance on this hearty and meaty veg.)

Celery

Eggplant

Fennel

Garlic

Gobo root (Also known as burdock root, gobo root is valued for its antibacterial, anti-inflammatory, and antioxidant properties. When peeled and cooked, it has a nutty and earthy flavor.)

Greens: kale, spinach, and beet tops

Mushrooms

Onions

Pumpkin and/or kabocha squash

Red bell peppers

Tomatoes (if unavailable, canned are OK)

Yams

FRUITS TO KEEP ON HAND WHEN IN SEASON

Fresh is best, but if using them for smoothies, frozen fruit is OK.

Apples

Avocado

Bananas

Blueberries

Dates (fresh or dried)

Mango

Strawberries

GRAINS, FLOURS, AND SEEDS

Almond flour

Barley

Bulgur wheat

Chia seeds

Chickpea flour

Farro

Flaxseeds

Ground flaxseed meal

Hemp seeds

Pumpkin seeds

Quinoa

Wheat berries

Unbleached organic all-purpose flour

NUTS

Almonds (raw)

Almonds (sliced)

Almonds (whole)

Cashews (whole raw)

Pecans (raw)

BEANS

I like to use dried beans and cook them myself (see page 84). Of course, we all want to be Martha Stewart, but if Martha isn't your thing, canned beans are just fine.

Black beans

Chickpeas

Great Northern white beans

Kidney beans

Pinto beans

SEASONINGS

Black pepper

Blackening spices

Cumin

Curry powder

Garlic powder

Himalayan pink salt (This specialty salt has a natural subtle sulfur flavor that when combined with certain ingredients resembles egg flavor.)

Kosher salt

Mirin (Japanese rice wine often used to provide a touch sweetness to sauces and dressings)

Nutritional yeast (A vegan staple that's great sprinkled on finished dishes—and popcorn—or added while cooking for a nutty, cheesy flavor.)

Miso paste (This is fermented soy bean paste. I know, sounds tasty, right? Miso has great health benefits, imparts an amazing umami flavor, and lasts a long time in fridge—which is great, because a little goes a long way.)

Onion powder

Oregano

Sake

Soy sauce or liquid aminos

OILS

Coconut oil

Extra-virgin olive oil

Grapeseed oil

Safflower oil

Toasted sesame oil

Vegan butter

ACID/VINEGARS

Apple cider vinegar

Balsamic vinegar

Champagne vinegar

Lemons and limes

Red wine vinegar

Seasoned rice vinegar

SWEETENERS

Real sugar is always better for you than artificial; just use less and your taste buds will adjust.

Agave syrup

Organic coconut sugar

Organic brown sugar

Organic white sugar

DRY GOOD STAPLES

Better Than Bouillon "No Beef" beef broth

Better Than Bouillon "No Chicken" chicken broth

Canned jackfruit

Nondairy milk: almond, soy, hemp, rice, or coconut

Tempeh bacon

Tofu (firm)

Vegan protein powder (see list and suggestions on page 60)

SUPERFOODS AND ANTIOXIDANTS

See page 60 for more info on these.

Camu powder

Fresh or frozen aloe vera pulp

Frozen acai berry pulp

Goji berry powder or dried berries

Maca powder

Maqui powder

Mulberry fruit powder

TOOLS

There are still many common misperceptions about cooking vegan. One of them is that you need all sorts of crazy gadgets and that you need to blow a ton of cash to outfit your kitchen. To that I say "Poppycock!" These basics will do right for all these recipes.

Food processor (OK, so these aren't cheap, but they are the only thing I recommend not skimping on. You can survive without a Vitamix or a KitchenAid stand mixer, but a Cuisinart food processor can become the most important tool in your kitchen—especially if you describe yourself as "chopping-impaired.")

A good set of bowls

A good sharp knife

Large colander

Large strainer

Mandolin (Optional, but nice to have. I prefer the plastic, Japanese-style mandolin, which incidentally is much less expensive than the large stainless-steel versions.)

Medium pot or soup pot

Rubber spatula

Salad spinner (optional, but nice to have)

Sauté pan

Skillet

Stockpot

Vegetable peeler

Wooden spoon

1

DIY BASICS, STAPLES, AND SAUCES THAT WILL CHANGE YOUR LIFE

(or at least your kitchen)

ROBERTO'S TOFU-RIZO

MAKES 1.5 CUPS

You can buy soy chorizo, but it's not nearly as good as homemade. This stuff is addictive! Add it to your favorite tofu scramble, make my Tacos de Pap con Chorizo (page 81), or add it to refried pinto or black beans for a quick, protein-packed bean burrito. Don't forget the Guacamole (page 27).

1 block extra-firm tofu

¼ cup apple cider vinegar

4 garlic cloves, minced

2 dried Ancho or Negro chiles

1 tablespoon chili powder

2 teaspoons kosher salt

1 teaspoon freshly ground black pepper

1 teaspoon dried oregano

1 teaspoon ground cumin

1 teaspoon ground coriander

3 whole cloves or ½ teaspoon ground

1 Cut the tofu into eight equal pieces lengthwise and lay them flat on a paper towel–lined kitchen towel. Cover the tofu with paper towels then place an additional kitchen towel over the tofu. Press down hard on the tofu to remove as much water as possible. (It's OK if the tofu bursts or crumbles a bit . . . keep squeezing.)

2 Push the tofu through a potato ricer into a medium bowl or chop the tofu up using a whisk or potato masher. Mix the vinegar and garlic into the tofu then set it aside.

3 Using a pair of scissors, cut the chiles open and remove the stem and seeds.

4 Cut the chiles into small pieces (about ½ to 1 inch) and place them in a food processor or spice grinder with the remaining ingredients and run the machine until the chiles are pulverized and the mixture is one blended spice.

5 Mix all the spices into the tofu mixture and stir until well combined. Place the tofu-rizo in a container with a tight-fitting lid.

TOFU-RIZO IS GOOD FOR 1 WEEK IN THE FRIDGE.

ALMOND-TOFU RICOTTA

MAKES 3 CUPS

This is an extremely versatile recipe. It plays a major role my Grilled Vegetable Lasagne (page 165) and in my Enchiladas (page 204). You can use this recipe anytime something calls for ricotta, and it can easily be flavored by folding in wilted spinach, sautéed mushrooms, fresh basil, chopped chives . . . I like it over sliced heirloom tomatoes with extra-virgin olive oil and balsamic.

---

1 cup whole blanched, sliced, or slivered almonds

1 block firm tofu

3 tablespoons nutritional yeast

1½ teaspoons garlic powder

1½ teaspoons onion powder

2 teaspoons Himalayan pink salt or kosher salt

PREPARE THE ALMONDS

1 Soak the almonds in water overnight or follow these steps: Bring 2 cups of water to a simmer. Remove the water from the heat and add the almonds. Allow the almonds to soak 45 minutes. Drain and rinse the almonds.

2 In a food processor, chop the almonds until smooth.

3 Place the almonds in two sheets of cheesecloth and squeeze the heck out of them. While the almonds are being squeezed tight remove the "milk" that emerges on the outside of the cloth with a rubber spatula. Place the pressed almonds in a bowl and reserve.

4 Cut the tofu block into eight equal slabs then squeeze the tofu between paper towel–lined kitchen towels until the slabs burst, removing as much liquid as possible.

5 Over a medium bowl, push the tofu through a potato ricer or crumble the tofu with your fingers then whisk the tofu in the bowl until it is smooth. Using a rubber spatula fold in the pressed almond mixture, yeast, and seasonings. At this point the almond ricotta is ready to be stored or used.

RICOTTA IS GOOD FOR 4 DAYS REFRIGERATED. I DO NOT RECOMMEND FREEZING.

ALMOND BACON BITS

MAKES 1 CUP

God only knows what commercially sold bacon bits are made of . . . I would never serve those to someone I love. Let's break it down: Real bacon is what? Salty, smoked protein and fat that has a crispy-crunchy texture when cooked. We have all those qualities here completely animal free and without the use of highly processed ingredients! In fact, these little morsels have only four ingredients, they are super easy to make—and I strongly advise that you make more than you need, because they will disappear quickly.

1 cup sliced almonds

1 teaspoon extra-virgin olive oil

1 teaspoon liquid smoke

½ teaspoon kosher salt

1 Place the almonds in a dry skillet and toast them over medium heat, agitating them constantly until light brown. Remove the almonds from the heat.

2 In a very small bowl mix the olive oil and liquid smoke, add it to the nuts, and toss. Mix in the kosher salt.

3 Return the almonds to the heat and continue tossing the almonds around the pan until they appear dry and a deep golden brown. Remove them from the heat and continue tossing until the pan cools off.

4 Place the almonds on a plate until completely cool. Store the nuts in an airtight container.

BACON BITS ARE GOOD FOR 3 WEEKS BUT THERE IS NO WAY YOU WILL HAVE THEM THAT LONG.

ALMOND FETA CHEESE

MAKES 8 SERVINGS

The most common comment I hear from people in terms of going vegan is that they don't want to give up cheese. I totally understand that desire. My wife and I have fond memories that involve some good-quality brie or goat cheese and a glass of red wine shared among friends. These are warm, fuzzy feelings that we have psychologically connected to food and there is no reason we should try to sever those connections. Instead, we bridge those memories with similar yet kinder and healthier great-tasting foods. This cheese is almond-based, creamy, and delicious—great as a spread for sandwiches or crackers.

4 cups whole blanched almonds

2 tablespoons lemon juice

¼ cup extra-virgin olive oil

4 garlic cloves, chopped

2 teaspoons kosher salt

TIP:

Want a great appetizer? This almond cheese pairs amazingly well with the Kalamata Olive and Basil Tapenade on page 32—it's the perfect thing to bring to the coffee table with a bottle of red or white wine, some crusty French bread, Marcona almonds, and some extra-virgin olive oil and balsamic vinegar drizzled on a large dinner plate. No reason to make an issue of being vegan here . . . just good food, good friends, and good times.

1 Soak the almonds in water overnight or follow these steps: Bring 4 cups of water to a simmer. Remove the water from the heat and add the almonds. Allow the almonds to soak 1 hour. Drain and rinse the almonds.

2 Using a food processor, chop the almonds, lemon juice, olive oil, garlic, and salt until smooth.

3 Line a medium bowl with two layers of cheesecloth. Be sure to use large pieces of cheesecloth so there is plenty to fold over the top.

4 Spoon the almond cheese into the cheesecloth-covered bowl. Bring the corners and sides of the cheesecloth together to form a sack and twist the top closed and keep twisting the cloth as tight as you can. While holding the cloth tight in one hand, use a rubber spatula to scrape the "milk" off the outside of the sack. Do this a few times.

5 Untwist the cheesecloth and scoop the almond feta into a bowl. Cover and refrigerate the cheese until cold.

6 When the cheese is cold, shape it into a square or circle on a platter about 1 inch thick.

THE CHEESE IS GOOD FOR 1 WEEK IN THE FRIDGE.

CASHEW CREAM

MAKES 3 CUPS

This is a vegan staple—a basic thick cream that you can use in recipes such as Classic Potatoes Gratin (page 153) and Not Your Grammy's Green Bean Casserole (page 154).

1½ cups raw organic cashews

2 cups water, plus more for soaking

1 Soak cashews in cool water overnight or follow these steps: Bring 3 cups of water to a simmer. Remove the water from the heat and add the cashews. Allow the cashews to soak 1 hour. Drain the soaking liquid and rinse the cashews.

2 Place the cashews in a blender and add water 4 inches above the cashews (about 2 cups). Blend until completely smooth, stopping a few times to scrape down the sides.

3 Strain the mixture to remove any particles that did not get pureed. Cashew cream should be the consistency of heavy cream.

CREAM IS GOOD FOR 1 WEEK REFRIGERATED OR 2 MONTHS FROZEN.

CHIPOTLE NUT CREAM

MAKES 1 CUP

This is another good basic. You can use it as a condiment à la sour cream (check out the Low-Carb Raw Taco Wraps on page 78) or as a dip for fries (Perfectly Baked Yam Fries, page 150). You can also use it to add kick to a burger or sandwich—it's a versatile sauce.

½ cup raw, blanched almonds, brought to a boil then soaked 15 minutes and strained

¼ cup extra-virgin olive oil or safflower oil

One 7-ounce can chipotle chiles in adobo sauce

Kosher salt to taste

1 In a food processor or blender, puree the almonds, olive oil, and 2 tablespoons of the thick liquid found in the can of chipotles until smooth (reserve the chiles and remaining sauce in an airtight container for another use).

2 Season the sauce with kosher salt and reserve in a squeeze bottle or small container.

SAUCE IS GOOD FOR 2 WEEKS REFRIGERATED.

PEPITAS *(Toasted Pumpkin Seeds)*

Many stores sell seasoned pepitas, and they make a great snack and salad topper. Toasting your own pumpkin seeds is a snap, so you'll have to forgive me for not giving you measurements here but you never know how many seeds you will get from a pumpkin, and some of you need to learn to cook without measurements. Let go of that recipe security blanket and trust your instincts.

Assuming you bought a pumpkin and don't want to throw away the seeds (and you shouldn't) here's the plan:

Pumpkin seeds

Extra-virgin olive oil to taste

Kosher salt to taste

Any flavors you might want to add!

1 Start by placing all the seeds in a large colander and remove as much of the pumpkin strings and guts as possible. Pick out any large pieces and rinse the seeds with cold water. (You will never get every little string and piece of pumpkin guts out; just go for the big ones.)

2 Spread the seeds out on a sheet tray and let them sit out for one day. You can stash them in an unheated oven if you like.

3 After the seeds have dried, toss them in a medium bowl, and drizzle with extra-virgin olive oil, and season with kosher salt. You can also jazz them up with some Cajun spice, curry, Old Bay, popcorn salt . . . do it up.

4 Preheat the oven to 275°F.

5 Spread the seeds out evenly on a clean sheet tray and bake them for 45 minutes to an hour, depending on the quantity. To keep them from cooking unevenly or burning, toss the seeds a bit halfway through the baking process. The shells will turn brown to pale green, depending on the pumpkin variety. When the seeds are toasted to perfection remove them from the oven and allow them to cool completely before storing.

PEPITAS WILL KEEP FOR A MONTH STORED IN AN AIRTIGHT CONTAINER (BUT THEY'LL GET EATEN LONG BEFORE THAT).

PICKLES

Not only is making your own pickles cheaper and healthier (no weird added preservatives or junk), it's also just a lot of fun (and if you don't think so, go ahead and put your kids to work). This method is known as the quick-pickle method, which is closer to a marinade because everything takes place in the fridge. No special canning equipment is needed and you can do this in Tupperware or an old jar. I like this method because, let's face it, who wants to wait weeks for anything? Also, we are going for flavor here, not preservation, so there's no risk of bacterial growth.

There are endless types of pickling but ultimately, we are always dealing with varying degrees of sweet, sour, salty, or spicy; after that it's a matter of seasonings. Here are a few recipes, but once you get the point you can tweak the ingredients and come up with your own "secret recipe."

NOTE:

If you are reusing a jar, make sure it has been cleaned with hot soapy water and inspect the lid to verify that it has no rust. A 1-quart mason jar or pasta sauce jar works best.

(CONTINUED) >

hamburger pickles

MAKES 1 QUART JAR OF PICKLES

The name says it all: these are great on any sandwich; they're also excellent in a salad for crunch and acidity.

4 cups pickling, Israeli, or Persian cucumbers, sliced ⅛ inch thick

1½ cups apple cider vinegar

⅓ cup organic white sugar

1 teaspoon kosher salt

1 teaspoon cracked peppercorns

1 tablespoon dill seeds

1 teaspoon mustard seeds

2 tablespoons fresh chopped dill

1 Place the sliced cumbers in a large jar or container with a tight-fitting lid.

2 In a small saucepan bring to a simmer the vinegar, sugar, salt, and peppercorns and stir until the salt and sugar have dissolved.

3 Pour the hot vinegar mixture over the cucumbers and add the dill seeds, mustard seeds, and dill.

4 Allow the pickles to cool uncovered for at least 1 hour or until room temperature. When cool, fit the lid on the container and shake vigorously to mix the seasoning and herbs.

5 Refrigerate the pickles for 2 days before eating.

PICKLES ARE GOOD FOR 2 WEEKS+ REFRIGERATED.

bread and butter pickles

MAKES 1 QUART JAR OF PICKLES

Although these sweet treats are great in sandwiches, I really like them on their own as a snack or served next to some quality olives and Marcona almonds . . . yeah, they are that good.

4 cups pickling, Israeli, or Persian cucumbers, washed and sliced ¼ inch+ thick

½ small red onion, sliced thin

1 medium red bell pepper, sliced thin

1½ cups apple cider vinegar

¾ cup organic white sugar

1 tablespoon kosher salt

1 tablespoon mustard seeds

1 teaspoon celery seeds

¼ teaspoon ground or crushed cloves

1 Place the sliced cumbers, onion, and bell pepper in a large jar or container with a tight-fitting lid.

2 In a small saucepan bring to a simmer the vinegar, sugar, and salt and stir until the salt and sugar have dissolved, about 5 minutes.

3 Pour the hot vinegar mixture over the vegetables and add the mustard seeds, celery seeds, and cloves.

4 Allow the pickles to cool uncovered for at least 1 hour or until room temperature. When cool, fit the lid on the container and shake vigorously to mix the seasoning and herbs.

5 Refrigerate the pickles for 2 days before eating.

PICKLES ARE GOOD FOR 2 WEEKS+ REFRIGERATED.

pickled cauliflower with lemon and chili

MAKES 1 QUART JAR OF PICKLED CAULIFLOWER

OMG you might eat these all in one sitting! Try them on the side of a one-pot meal like Baingan Bhartha (page 201).

1 large cauliflower head

1 small lemon, cut in wedges

3 large garlic cloves, sliced

1½ cups apple cider vinegar

2 teaspoons chili powder

2 teaspoons sea salt

¼ teaspoon peppercorns

3 tablespoons maple syrup

Water as needed

1 Cut the cauliflower head into small florets and cut the heart and stems into similar size pieces.

2 Bring a large pot of water to a rolling boil and season it with two big pinches of kosher salt. Par-cook the cauliflower florets and stem pieces until just barely tender (about 2 minutes).

3 Drain the cauliflower and quickly place it in a 1-quart jar or container with a tight-fitting lid.

4 Squeeze the lemon wedges over the cauliflower and place the squeezed wedges in the jar with the cauliflower. Add the garlic, vinegar, chili powder, salt, peppercorns, and syrup. If necessary, pour as much water as needed to cover the cauliflower.

5 Allow the cauliflower to cool uncovered for at least 1 hour or until room temperature. When cool, fit the lid on the jar and shake vigorously to mix the seasoning and herbs.

6 Refrigerate the pickles for 2 days before eating.

PICKLES ARE GOOD FOR 2 WEEKS+ REFRIGERATED.

escabeche (pickled onions and jalapeños)

MAKES 1 QUART JAR OF ESCABECHE

Growing up in a Latino household meant there was always a large bowl of escabeche on the table. I love this spicy pickled salad; it acts as a refreshing palate cleanser and food topper. One might call it a Mexican kimchi. You know you are in an authentic taqueria when there is a big, help-yourself bowl of escabeche off to the side of the register. Sometimes they put cooked potato in it but I don't go for those kinds of shenanigans. Serve this on the side with the Tacos de Papa con Chorizo (page 81) or the Jackfruit Soft Tacos in Guajillo Sauce (page 207).

3 tablespoons extra-virgin olive oil

1 large white onion, thinly sliced

3 fat carrots, peeled and cut in ⅛-inch slices

4 jalapeños, thinly sliced crosswise
(retain seeds)

½ cup water

2 tablespoons dried oregano

1 teaspoon kosher salt

1 tablespoon sugar

1 cup apple cider vinegar

½ cup white distilled vinegar

1 Heat a large skillet or sauté pan over medium-high heat. Add the olive oil to the pan and wait for it to shimmer.

2 Add the onions, carrots, and jalapeños and stir with a wooden spoon until the onions are translucent, about 5 minutes. Carefully add the water and bring the liquid to a simmer. Add the oregano, salt, and sugar to the onions then remove the pan from the heat.

3 Place the onion mixture in a 1-quart jar or container with a tight-fitting lid. Pour the vinegars over the onion mixture. Allow the escabeche to cool uncovered for at least 1 hour or until room temp.

4 When cool, fit the lid on the container and shake vigorously to mix the seasoning and herbs.

5 Refrigerate the salad for 2 days before eating.

THESE PICKLES ARE GOOD FOR 2 WEEKS+ REFRIGERATED.

BASIC GUACAMOLE

Who doesn't like guacamole? (Well, some people don't, but let's agree those people are deranged.) This super-basic recipe is perfect for tacos; if I'm busting out the chips I always add diced tomato, red onion, and cilantro. Another great thing about guac: it's super easy—you can make it free form . . . a little of this, a dash of that, taste and adjust. Few foods are as correctable as guacamole; even if it's too salty, more avocado will fix it right up.

2 ripe avocados

½ medium lime, juiced

½ teaspoon ground cumin

1 teaspoon garlic powder

1 teaspoon onion powder

Kosher salt and freshly ground black pepper to taste

3 firm Roma tomatoes, hearts and seeds removed, diced small (optional)

¼ red onion, minced (optional)

½ bunch cilantro, stems included, roughly chopped (optional)

1 Carefully score the avocado all the way around the pit and twist the halves apart. Remove the pit and use a large spoon to scrape the flesh out of the skin into a medium bowl.

2 Add the remaining ingredients and mash the avocado with a large whisk or fork. (Note: Mash the avocado before adding the tomatoes, onions, and cilantro, if using.)

ALTHOUGH GUACAMOLE IS AT ITS BEST THE DAY IT IS MADE, IT WILL LAST 2–3 DAYS REFRIGERATED IN AN AIRTIGHT CONTAINER.

SALSA *de* JITOMATE ASADO
(Roasted Tomato Salsa)

MAKES 2 CUPS

This may take a little more time than your standard-issue salsa, but the depth of flavor from roasting the tomatoes is totally worth it. This is great with tacos, tofu scrambles, or any dish that needs a little help in the flavor department.

4 large tomatoes, cored and halved

4 garlic cloves

1 small red onion, chopped in large pieces

3 green or red jalapeños, seeded and chopped in large pieces

1 bunch cilantro, stems included, finely chopped

1 lime, juiced

1 teaspoon ground cumin

1 tablespoon dried oregano

Kosher salt and freshly ground black pepper

1 Preheat oven to 475°F or heat the broiler.

2 Place the tomatoes skin side up on a foil-lined sheet tray and hide the garlic under one of the tomato halves. Scatter the onions and jalapeños among the tomatoes.

3 Bake for about 20 minutes or until the tomatoes and onions are charred. (They'll need about 8 to 10 minutes in the broiler.) Remove from heat and allow the tomatoes to cool.

4 Separate the tomatoes from the onions, peppers, and garlic, and peel off their skins.

5 Place the onions, peppers, and garlic in a food processor and pulse until they are chopped small, stopping a few times to scrape down the sides of the container. Place the onion mixture in a medium bowl.

6 Put the tomatoes in the food processor and pulse until almost smooth.

7 Stir the tomatoes, cilantro, lime juice, cumin, and oregano into the onion mixture and season with salt and pepper.

8 Allow the salsa to cool before storing in an airtight container in the refrigerator.

SALSA IS GOOD FOR 1 WEEK REFRIGERATED OR 2 MONTHS FROZEN.

SALSA *de* TOMATILLO ASADO
(Roasted Tomatillo Salsa)

MAKES ABOUT 3 CUPS

Tomatillos are the small green tomatoes encased in husks. They're not difficult to work with but require a little extra time to remove the sticky film that rests on their skin. There is no substitute for tomatillos; their flavor is unique. They possess a subtle earthy/lime flavor that, partnered with vinegar and cumin, becomes something really special. This salsa's so delicious you can use it in place of a salad dressing.

1 pound fresh tomatillos, husked and washed in cool water until no longer sticky

1 large white or yellow onion, cut into large chunks

6 garlic cloves, whole

2 green jalapeños, halved and seeded, stems removed

2 tablespoons extra-virgin olive oil

1 bunch cilantro, stems included, chopped

2 tablespoons red wine vinegar

1 tablespoon ground cumin

1 teaspoon dried oregano

Kosher salt as needed

1 Preheat the broiler and line a sheet tray with foil.

2 Cut the tomatillos in half lengthwise and toss them in a large bowl with the onions, garlic, and jalapeños. Add the olive oil and toss until well coated.

3 Arrange the tomatillos and jalapeños skin side up on the sheet tray and top them with the onions and garlic.

4 Broil the vegetables for 5 to 7 minutes or until they are soft and blistered. Remove them from the broiler and allow them to cool.

5 Carefully hold the edges of the foil and pour the roasted vegetables into the food processor. Add the cilantro, vinegar, cumin, and oregano and pulse the salsa about five times then scrape down sides and run the food processor for about 10 seconds. The salsa should be chopped uniformly with a few larger chunks here and there. Season aggressively with salt.

6 Allow the salsa to cool before storing in an airtight container in the refrigerator.

SALSA IS GOOD FOR 1 WEEK.

SALSA MOJADA

MAKES 2 CUPS

Salsa mojada means "wet sauce." This is the to-mato-based mild salsa that goes with or on every-thing. It is quick and easy to make and it lasts a long time. It is the perfect chip companion. Next time you make a quick veggie burrito, place it on an oven-safe plate then douse the top with this salsa and place it in a hot oven just long enough to heat the burrito and get the salsa hot. You now have a burrito mojado to enjoy.

½ small white onion, chopped

2 large vine-ripe tomatoes, core removed but left whole

2 red jalapeños, ribs and seeds removed

2 garlic cloves, crushed

Juice of 1 lime

1 tablespoon dried oregano

½ teaspoon sugar

½ bunch cilantro, stems included, chopped

Kosher salt to taste

1 In a medium saucepan bring 4 cups of wa-ter to a boil then add the onion, tomatoes, and jalapeños and simmer until the vegeta-bles are softened, about 10 minutes. Drain the water and allow the vegetables to cool.

2 Puree the cooked onions, tomatoes, and jalapeños in a food processor or blender with the garlic, lime juice, oregano, and sugar un-til the salsa is almost smooth. Add the cilan-tro and pulse until blended only.

3 Season the salsa with salt to taste.

4 Allow the salsa to cool before storing in an airtight container in the refrigerator.

SALSA IS GOOD FOR 1 WEEK REFRIGERATED.

KALAMATA OLIVE
and BASIL TAPENADE

MAKES 3 CUPS

Although insanely good over the Almond Feta Cheese (page 15), this spread is yummy enough to serve on its own with some pita bread. You can also serve it with French bread and a plate drizzled with extra-virgin olive oil.

---

2 red bell peppers, seeded and sliced into ¼-inch strips

2 tablespoons plus ¼ cup extra-virgin olive oil

1½ cups kalamata olives, pitted

1½ cups large green olives, pitted

4 garlic cloves, minced

10 large basil leaves, chopped

1 tablespoon dried oregano

2 tablespoons capers, drained

Freshly ground black pepper to taste

1 Toss the peppers in a bowl with 2 tablespoons olive oil.

2 Heat a grill pan or cast-iron pan blazing hot and grill/sear the peppers, stirring frequently until they are soft, wilted, and charred, about 10 minutes.

3 Place peppers and remaining ingredients in a food processor and pulse to combine, stopping to scrape down the sides of the bowl until the mixture becomes a coarse chopped salsa, about 1 to 2 minutes total.

4 Stir and season with black pepper.

STORED IN THE REFRIGERATOR IN A GLASS CONTAINER WITH A TIGHT-FITTING LID, THIS TAPENADE WILL KEEP FOR 2 WEEKS.

ROASTED RED PEPPER DIP

MAKES ABOUT 2½ CUPS

Tired of seeing ranch dressing and jarred salsa on the table? Bring this to the next get-together and watch it disappear. This is not just another red pepper dip, either. The mango adds a very different note of sweetness and complexity that complements the charred-red-pepper smokiness. Do you like a little heat? Add a tablespoon of chili powder to kick it up a notch. Serve with corn chips, your favorite bread, pita, or raw veggies.

6 large red bell peppers

1 ripe mango, peeled and chopped

¼ cup extra-virgin olive oil

2 teaspoons chopped fresh oregano or 1 teaspoon dried

Juice of 1 lemon

Kosher salt and freshly ground black pepper to taste

1 Wash and dry the peppers well then place them directly over a high flame, two peppers per burner. (If you don't have a gas stove, see broiler instructions in the note below.) Turn the peppers with a pair of metal tongs to char all sides. When all surfaces of the peppers are black, place the peppers in a large bowl and cover the bowl to steam the skins.

2 Rub the black skin off the peppers with a paper towel. If you didn't use the broiler, remove the seeds but try to save any liquid that has accumulated in the pepper.

3 Roughly chop the skinned peppers and place them in a food processor with the remaining ingredients. Run the machine until the dip is smooth and airy.

4 Season well with salt and pepper. Serve immediately or save in an airtight container and refrigerate.

DIP IS GOOD FOR 4 DAYS+ REFRIGERATED.

NOTE:

To roast peppers using your broiler, cut the peppers in half lengthwise and remove the seeds and membrane. Preheat the broiler and place the peppers cut side down on a sheet tray. Broil the peppers until the skins turn black and blistered, about 4 minutes. Place the peppers in a large bowl and cover the bowl to steam the skins. Proceed with the instructions as noted.

PECAN PESTO

While pine nuts are the de rigueur ingredient in pesto, I love using pecans instead; they have a more complex and hearty flavor. Try this pesto with pasta, in soups, as a sandwich spread, or mixed in hummus.

2 ounces fresh basil or about 45 leaves, washed and dried

2 ounces (¾ cup) raw pecan pieces

2 tablespoons nutritional yeast (optional)

½ teaspoon kosher salt

5 garlic cloves, crushed

¾ cup extra-virgin olive oil

Kosher salt and freshly ground black pepper to taste

1 Put all ingredients in a food processor and let it run until smooth. Stop three or four times to scrape down the sides.

2 Season with salt and pepper.

3 Refrigerate immediately.

PESTO IS GOOD FOR 1 WEEK REFRIGERATED.

WASABI AIOLI

This is one of my favorite sauces, hands down. Sauces and dressings have come and gone but I still enjoy this one as much as the first time I made it. It's a part of me, a window into my culinary soul and now . . . I give it you . . . "Don't mess it up!"

I use this dressing in my Blackened Plum Tomatoes over Cucumber and Fennel Salad (page 136). After you make this Wasabi Aioli you're going to look for an excuse to put it on something, it's just so good. I like to use it as a salad dressing or as a brown rice topper.

1 cup Basic Mayo (page 36), or store-bought vegan mayonnaise

½ cup reduced-sodium soy sauce

Juice of 3 limes

3 tablespoons prepared wasabi

2 bunches cilantro, washed and bottom 1 inch of stems removed

1 bunch scallions (green parts only)

1 garlic clove, crushed

1 Place everything in a blender and puree until smooth.

2 Save in an airtight container or squeeze bottle and refrigerate.

SAUCE IS GOOD FOR 1 WEEK.

BASIC MAYO

MAKES 2 CUPS

Like homemade ketchup, making your own vegan mayonnaise is a snap and it's cheaper than buying it. Below is the basic recipe for mayonnaise, but you can season it with anything to make it your own. I've offered some suggestions, but really, the sky's the limit.

½ cup unsweetened almond milk

1 tablespoon Dijon mustard

1 teaspoon organic sugar

2 tablespoons lemon juice

1 teaspoon kosher salt

1¼ cups grapeseed or safflower oil

¼ cup ground flaxseeds or flaxseed meal

1 Put the almond milk, mustard, sugar, lemon juice, and salt in a blender or food processor and puree.

2 With the blender running on medium speed, very slowly pour in the oil.

3 After all of the oil has been poured, add the flaxseed and run the blender about three seconds more to incorporate. The mixture will be a thick liquid. Pour the mixture in a jar or other airtight container and refrigerate. This mayonnaise will thicken and stabilize once it has been chilled.

MAYONNAISE IS GOOD FOR 2 MONTHS REFRIGERATED.

TIP

Here are some flavoring ideas; you can add these ingredients along with the ground flaxseeds:

- 1 roasted red bell pepper, chopped
- 1 tablespoon wasabi
- 2 tablespoons minced garlic
- 1 bunch cilantro, minced
- 1 bunch basil, minced
- 1 bunch chives, minced
- 2 tablespoons sun-dried tomato paste
- 2 tablespoons Sriracha
- 2 tablespoons extra lemon juice + 2 tablespoons capers
- 2 tablespoons chipotle sauce
- 10 pitted Kalamata olives, chopped

NO-FUSS KETCHUP

MAKES 3 CUPS

Ketchup is one of those things that we often buy because it's cheap and easy to grab the bottle. Guess what? It's even cheaper and pretty easy to make. Bonus: you'll know exactly what's in it. Bonus 2: for some reason when I make my own it doesn't seem like such a lame condiment.

1¼ cups apple cider vinegar

2 teaspoons salt

½ large white onion, chopped

4 garlic cloves, chopped

Two 6-ounce cans organic tomato paste

¾ cup organic brown sugar (or less if desired)

1 Add all the ingredients to a blender, puree until smooth, and pour into a glass jar or container. That's it! You made ketchup.

KETCHUP IS GOOD FOR 2 MONTHS REFRIGERATED.

BASIC TOMATO SAUCE

MAKES 3½ CUPS

Fresh tomatoes and canned tomatoes make very different sauces. I like them both depending on what the sauce is going to be used for. This quick sauce is vibrant and perfect for Eggplant Parm (page 167) while a richer, longer-stewed sauce, like the Simple and Best Marinara Sauce (page 43), might be more appropriate for a different dish.

2 tablespoons extra-virgin olive oil

1 white onion, diced small

6 garlic cloves, sliced

¾ cup red wine

10 Roma tomatoes, roasted, peeled, and diced (see method on page 40)

2 tablespoons chopped parsley

¼ cup chopped basil

Kosher salt and freshly ground black pepper to taste

1 In a 3 to 4–quart saucepan, heat the olive oil over medium heat.

2 Add the onion and garlic and cook until they are soft and light golden brown, about 10 minutes. Stir the onions occasionally with a wooden spoon.

3 Add the wine and simmer until reduced by half, about 8 minutes.

4 Add the tomatoes and bring the sauce to a boil. Reduce the heat to medium-low and simmer the sauce for about 15 minutes uncovered. Stir in the parsley and basil.

5 Carefully puree the sauce in a blender until smooth. Season with salt and pepper.

SAUCE IS GOOD FOR 1 WEEK REFRIGERATED OR 4 MONTHS FROZEN.

TOMATOES: EASY-PEEL METHOD

MAKES THE EQUIVALENT OF A 14.5-OUNCE CAN CRUSHED OR DICED TOMATOES

Have you ever read a so-called "easy" recipe that called for peeling fresh tomatoes? Yeah, "Concasse? No thank you!"—that's what I say. I think that the basic thought of peeling fresh tomatoes is what encourages most people to reach for the jar. The classic method is to core, score, and simmer the tomatoes then shock them in ice water, remove the skins then cut and dice the tomatoes . . . Sheesh! I'm pretty fast and I don't like doing all that. Especially when I only need eight tomatoes' worth. That's why I came up with this quick method that actually enhances the tomato flavor. This technique can be used any time a recipe calls for canned whole, stewed, diced, or chopped tomatoes.

---

5 to 6 Roma tomatoes

Drizzle of extra-virgin olive oil

1 Preheat the oven to 500°F or turn on the broiler. Lightly oil a sheet tray and set it aside.

2 Cut the tomatoes in half lengthwise bisecting the core. Holding your knife at a sharp angle cut out the core from each half. Lay the tomato halves cut-side down on the oiled sheet tray.

3 Bake or broil the tomatoes just long enough to scorch the skins, about 3 to 5 minutes depending on the oven. (Note: Cooking time may be as long as 8 minutes if peeling a full sheet tray of tomatoes.) Remove the tomatoes from the oven and allow them to cool slightly on the baking sheet.

4 Using a pair of tongs or your fingers (depending on how hot the tomatoes are) you can pull the skins off easily in one piece.

5 Once the tomatoes are peeled follow the recipe instructions, for example if the recipe calls for crushed tomatoes, crush the peeled tomatoes by hand. If the recipe calls for diced tomatoes then dice the peeled tomatoes. Be sure to get all the juices from the sheet tray and cutting board (if used) into the final product.

PEELED TOMATOES ARE GOOD FOR 5 DAYS IF HELD IN AN AIRTIGHT CONTAINER AND REFRIGERATED.

TIP:

If you have an abundance of fresh tomatoes, peel them using this method then freeze the peeled halves in resealable plastic bags. Lay the bags flat and thin rather than in a large block; this allows you to defrost the tomatoes quickly and break off only as much as you need.

SIMPLE *and* BEST MARINARA SAUCE

MAKES ABOUT 6 CUPS

This is the easiest and best-tasting pasta sauce you will ever make. Having this sauce in your fridge or freezer can get you out of a jam. Toss it with penne or spaghetti and you are a salad and garlic bread away from having dinner on the table.

⅓ cup extra-virgin olive oil

1 large white or yellow onion, diced medium

6 garlic cloves, crushed

1 teaspoon dried oregano

½ teaspoon kosher salt

½ teaspoon crushed red pepper

1 cup red wine like Chianti or Merlot

Two 28-ounce cans good-quality crushed tomatoes (San Marzano are the best) or 22 Roma tomatoes, peeled using the easy-peel method (page 40)

1 handful fresh flat-leaf parsley leaves, chopped

10 to 15 large fresh basil leaves, chopped

Kosher salt and freshly ground black pepper to taste

1 Heat a large saucepan over high heat then add the olive oil and wait for it to shimmer.

2 Add the onions and cook until soft and light brown (about 6 minutes). Add the garlic, oregano, salt, and red pepper and cook 1 minute more.

3 Carefully add the wine and simmer until reduced by half, about 5 minutes. Stir in the tomatoes and return the sauce to a simmer. Continue to simmer the marinara uncovered over low heat until it thickens, about 45 minutes to 1 hour. Stir the sauce once in awhile to prevent scorching.

4 Remove the sauce from heat and stir in the parsley and basil and season with salt and pepper to taste.

5 Puree the sauce with an immersion blender or regular blender just enough to make all the chunks the same size (do not make it smooth).

MARINARA IS GOOD FOR A WEEK REFRIGERATED OR 3 MONTHS FROZEN.

CILANTRO CHIMICHURRI SAUCE

MAKES ABOUT 2 CUPS

You'll want to plan ahead with this sauce, since it really is so much better the next day. The raw garlic and onion mellows out and the acidity of the vinegar and lemon juice subsides to create a flavor that's distinct but not overpowering. If you have the opportunity to make it in advance, it is worth the wait (if not, it is still enjoyable). Try it over grilled tofu steaks, grilled vegetables, or on my Black Bean Mushroom Burger (page 82).

6 large garlic cloves, minced

½ small red onion, minced

½ cup red wine vinegar

Juice of 1 lemon

1 cup extra-virgin olive oil

1 tablespoon dried oregano

1 teaspoon smoked paprika

1 bunch fresh cilantro, stems included, chopped fine

1 bunch fresh flat-leaf parsley, leaves only, chopped fine

2 teaspoons kosher salt

Freshly ground black pepper to taste

1 Mix all of the ingredients in a medium bowl, cover, and let the sauce sit at room temperature for about 2 hours before refrigerating.

THE SAUCE IS GOOD FOR 2 WEEKS REFRIGERATED.

SWEET SOY GLAZE

MAKES 1½ CUPS

Sweet-savory flavor combinations are always a treat. I use this sauce in my recipe for Blackened Plum Tomatoes over Cucumber Salad (page 136), but you can also enjoy it drizzled over brown rice or mixed with Dijon mustard for a killer salad dressing. It can really elevate your vegetables; try it poured over roasted pieces of sweet potato and butternut squash and chopped sage.

1 cup reduced-sodium soy sauce

1 teaspoon cornstarch

¾ cup brown sugar or organic coconut sugar

½ teaspoon freshly ground black pepper

1 Place all the ingredients in a small saucepan over medium-high heat and whisk until the sugar is dissolved. Watch the sauce carefully and remove it from the heat as soon as it starts to simmer. Whisk the sauce a little more and allow it to cool.

2 When the sauce is no longer hot, store it in a squeeze bottle or a small glass jar.

SOY GLAZE IS GOOD FOR 1 MONTH REFRIGERATED.

BOURBON BBQ SAUCE

MAKES ABOUT 3 CUPS

This stuff is the backbone of my Bad Boy Pulled Barbecue Sandwiches (page 85), but you can slather it on anything you want to give that sweet and smoky kiss. If you want to intensify the flavor, a few tablespoons of Sriracha, chili powder, or chipotles would be great here, too.

2 cups No-Fuss Ketchup (page 38), or store-bought vegan ketchup

⅓ cup maple syrup

¼ cup apple cider vinegar

¼ cup soy sauce

4 ounces bourbon

Zest of 1 orange

Juice of 2 large oranges

Zest and juice of 1 lemon

2 teaspoons liquid smoke

1 tablespoon onion powder (not onion salt!)

½ teaspoon freshly ground black pepper or more if desired

6 garlic cloves, chopped

1 Place all the ingredients in a blender and puree until smooth.

2 Pour the sauce into a small saucepan and bring to a gentle simmer over medium heat. Simmer the sauce for about 25 minutes or until it has thickened. Remove the sauce from the heat and let it cool.

3 Store the sauce in a glass jar or good container and refrigerate.

SAUCE IS GOOD FOR 1 MONTH—IF YOU CAN KEEP YOUR HANDS OFF IT THAT LONG.

FILIPINO BBQ SAUCE

MAKES 2¼ CUPS

As a southern California native and as a private chef I have befriended many good peeps from the Philippines. I picked up this recipe from a former coworker who was always sharing recipes with me. Be forewarned: when this sauce hits the grill it puts out a sweet and savory aroma that is nothing short of intoxicating. I'd eat a kitchen towel that was grilled in this sauce.

Here are just a few ideas of how to use this sauce on the grill: cauliflower skewers, eggplant slices, pineapple wedges, Gardein skewers, vegetable kabobs . . . It truly is versatile. Be sure to have some sauce left over to drizzle on steamed rice.

1 cup water

½ cup reduced-sodium soy sauce

½ cup apple cider vinegar

¼ cup orange juice

Juice of 1 lemon

½ cup brown sugar

2 tablespoons molasses

1 tablespoon tomato paste

1 medium white onion, minced

6 garlic cloves, minced

One 1-inch piece fresh ginger, peeled and minced

2 teaspoons freshly ground black pepper

1 teaspoon chili powder

1 Put all the ingredients a saucepan over medium-low heat and bring to a simmer while whisking.

2 Allow the sauce to simmer 5 to 8 minutes then remove from the heat to cool. Store in a glass jar or container in the refrigerator.

THE SAUCE WILL KEEP FOR 1 MONTH.

ORANGE GASTRIQUE

MAKES 1 CUP

A gastrique is fancy word for sweet and sour sauce. Classically, it is paired with fatty foods like duck or lamb; the acid (sour flavor) helps cut the fat. Nowadays it is used on and in all kinds of things including some hipster cocktails. I put together this recipe to use the gastrique as a marinade/dressing for my Shaved Fennel with Arugula Crunch Salad (page 135). The acid helps to soften the fennel and the sweetness balances the peppery arugula, but you could also use the sauce on roasted beets, grilled vegetables, or anything that has avocado in it. It's a great sauce to have in your repertoire.

¼ cup brown sugar

¼ cup maple syrup

½ cup apple cider vinegar

Zest and juice of 2 large oranges

2 whole cloves

1 cinnamon stick or 1 teaspoon ground cinnamon

2 garlic cloves, crushed

1 Whisk together all the ingredients in a medium saucepan and then bring the liquid to a simmer over medium heat.

2 Adjust the heat to low and simmer uncovered until the liquid reduces by half, about ¾ cup; this should take about 15 minutes.

3 Strain the gastrique and store it in a small bowl for immediate use.

4 Store any leftover gastrique in an airtight container in the fridge.

THE GASTRIQUE IS GOOD FOR 2 WEEKS REFRIGERATED.

BASIC VINAIGRETTE

MAKES ¾ CUP

This simple vinaigrette should be thought of as a base for all other vinaigrettes. You can substitute the red wine vinegar with champagne, apple cider, or white balsamic vinegar. Any number of chopped herbs may be added like tarragon, chive, basil, thyme, or sage. Keep this on hand to dress up a simple green salad or toss with veggies.

---

1 small shallot, minced

Juice of ½ lemon

2 tablespoons red wine vinegar

1 tablespoon Dijon mustard (I like Grey Poupon)

¼ cup extra-virgin olive oil

Kosher salt and freshly ground black pepper

1 In a medium bowl, whisk together all the ingredients and season well with salt and pepper.

2 Pour into a glass jar or other container (if you have a small mason jar handy you can put everything in the jar, screw the lid on tight, and shake vigorously); chill before using.

VINAIGRETTE IS GOOD FOR 1 WEEK REFRIGERATED.

BEET SALAD VINAIGRETTE

MAKES ABOUT 1 CUP

While I use this dressing for the Chopped Beet Salad with Beet Tops (page 124), this vinaigrette is also great for heartier greens like kale, endive, baby romaine, and arugula.

2 tablespoons Dijon mustard

4 tablespoons apple cider vinegar

2 tablespoons maple syrup

¼ cup extra-virgin olive oil

2 shallots, minced

Kosher salt and freshly ground black pepper

1 In a medium bowl, whisk together all the ingredients and season to taste with salt and pepper.

2 Pour into a glass jar or other container (if you have a small mason jar handy you can put everything in the jar, screw the lid on tight, and shake vigorously); chill before using.

VINAIGRETTE IS GOOD FOR 2 WEEKS REFRIGERATED.

KILLER BLOOD ORANGE VINAIGRETTE

Along with being the perfect companion to my Herbaceous and Nutty Wheat Berry Salad (page 127), this vinaigrette can not only jazz up the simplest of greens, but it's terrific on anything with avocado. Try it drizzled over your favorite cooked grains too.

Zest and juice of 2 blood oranges

2 medium shallots, minced

2 tablespoons balsamic vinegar

½ cup extra-virgin olive oil

½ teaspoon kosher salt

1 teaspoon freshly ground black pepper

1 sprig fresh thyme, leaves only, chopped

2 tablespoons Cointreau, Grand Marnier, or (if you must) triple sec

1 In a medium bowl, whisk together all the ingredients.

2 Pour into a glass jar or other container (if you have a small mason jar handy you can put everything in the jar, screw the lid on tight, and shake vigorously); chill before using.

VINAIGRETTE IS GOOD FOR 1 WEEK REFRIGERATED.

MEDITERRANEAN DRESSING

MAKES 1 CUP

This dressing goes perfectly with the Grilled Napa Salad (page 123); you can also use it to make your own Greek salad.

Juice of ½ lemon

2 tablespoons red wine vinegar

3 tablespoons extra-virgin olive oil, plus more as needed

3 large garlic cloves, minced

1 bunch flat-leaf parsley, leaves only, chopped

10 basil leaves, chopped

1 teaspoon dried oregano

Kosher salt and freshly ground black pepper to taste

1 In a medium bowl whisk all the dressing ingredients together and season with salt and pepper.

2 Pour into a glass jar or other container (if you have a small mason jar handy you can put everything in the jar, screw the lid on tight, and shake vigorously); chill before using.

THE DRESSING WILL KEEP IN THE REFRIGERATOR FOR 1 WEEK.

MISO DRESSING

MAKES 1 CUP

This dressing really is the finishing touch on the Beet Carpaccio with Arugula and Miso Dressing (page 126), but it's also a great dressing for any tender green lettuce like red leaf, butter lettuce, or baby romaine. If you're new to miso, it's a traditional Japanese seasoning made of fermented soybeans (trust me, it's much tastier than it sounds) that adds a salty-sweet kick. You can find miso in most natural grocery stores and Asian specialty markets.

2 shallots, minced

2 teaspoons Dijon mustard

Juice of ½ lemon

2 tablespoons organic brown sugar
or agave syrup

¼ cup shiro miso

3 tablespoons extra-virgin olive oil

One 1-inch piece fresh ginger,
peeled and minced

Freshly ground black pepper

1 In a medium bowl whisk all the dressing ingredients together and season with pepper.

2 Pour into a glass jar or other container (if you have a small mason jar handy you can put everything in the jar, screw the lid on tight, and shake vigorously); chill before using.

THE DRESSING WILL KEEP IN THE REFRIGERATOR FOR 1 WEEK.

GARLIC OIL

Garlic oil is very versatile. It can be used in place of extra-virgin olive oil in any dressing, drizzled over soups, or used as a marinade for grilled vegetables.

2 cups extra-virgin olive oil

12 garlic cloves, whole

1 teaspoon kosher salt

1 Place the olive oil and garlic cloves in a small saucepan over low heat for 25 minutes. Monitor the garlic; golden brown is OK but don't let the cloves fry or get dark.

2 When done, turn off the heat and allow to cool. When the oil is cool, puree the oil and garlic with the kosher salt until it is completely smooth.

3 Strain the oil into a container or squeeze bottle.

THE OIL WILL KEEP FOR 2 WEEKS IN THE REFRIGERATOR.

NOTE:

The oil will most likely solidify in the fridge, but it only takes about 5 minutes on the counter to be melted and ready.

BASIL OIL

MAKES 3 CUPS

Herb oils are often made by heating the ingredients in order to infuse their flavor into the oil. The whole thing is a bit unnecessary and hoity-toity to me. The flavor is often faint and a lot of oil is wasted in the straining process. By contrast, my technique is very uncomplicated and results in a really robust flavor.

Drizzle your herb oil on veggies before you grill them or after you've sautéed them. You can serve this oil drizzled on a big plate with crusty bread as a dipper or substitute this oil in any vinaigrette recipe that calls for extra-virgin olive oil. Basil oil is beautiful and delicious drizzled over your favorite soup just before serving.

15 fresh basil leaves, chopped

2½ cups extra-virgin olive oil

6 garlic cloves, crushed

1 teaspoon kosher salt

1 teaspoon freshly ground black pepper

1 Bring 4 cups of water to a boil.

2 Place the basil in a fine mesh strainer and hold the strainer over the sink. Slowly pour the boiling water over the basil. Place the basil in the center of two paper towels and squeeze them dry.

3 Place the olive oil in the blender. Add the basil, garlic, salt, and pepper. Puree until the oil is a light green with only unidentifiable specks of herbs. The oil will have a strong raw garlic flavor; this will mellow out in a few hours.

4 Pour the oil in a squeeze bottle or glass jar with a lid and keep refrigerated.

THE OIL WILL KEEP IN THE REFRIGERATOR FOR 3 WEEKS.

NOTES:

The oil will most likely solidify in the fridge but it only takes about 5 minutes on the counter to be melted and ready.

If you're not into basil, you can create any mixed herb oil with this recipe. Simply add your favorite fresh herbs to the existing recipe or omit the basil and use whatever you want.

CURRY POWDER

If you have access to a spice store, I highly recommend you start visiting. You can buy in small quantities, which allows you to experiment with the cool, unusual ingredients you'll find there. Making your own curry might seem like a bit much, but it is actually fun; plus, if you take the time to make it yourself, you are more likely to use it. You can also control the amount of heat in your curry, which might open some doors for the "too spicy" people in your house.

2 tablespoons coriander seeds

2 tablespoons cumin seeds

2 tablespoons cardamom seeds

2 teaspoons fennel seeds

2 teaspoons mustard seeds

½ teaspoon whole cloves

3 tablespoons turmeric

2 tablespoons chili powder (straight chili powder, not chili seasoning)

1 tablespoon cinnamon

1 Heat a dry skillet or sauté pan over medium heat.

2 Add the coriander, cumin, cardamom, fennel, mustard seeds, and cloves and toast the spices gently, shaking the pan occasionally, until they become aromatic and a few begin to pop, about 1 to 2 minutes. Remove from the heat.

3 Allow the spices to cool then place them in a coffee/spice grinder or mortar and pestle. Grind the spices into a fine powder. Pour them into a jar and mix in the turmeric, chili powder, and cinnamon.

STORED IN A COOL, DRY PLACE, CURRY IS GOOD FOR 2 MONTHS.

2

GET YOUR MORNING ON: SMOOTHIES AND OTHER BREAKFAST GOODNESS

SMOOTHIES *and* PROTEIN SHAKES

I'm a smoothie nut! I make them all the time at home. With smoothies, the possibilities really are endless. Here are some of my favorite flavor combos, along some suggestions for easy add-ins to amp up the nutrients.

All of these smoothies will make delicious frozen popsicles, too. If you don't have the molds, use paper cups, ice trays, or hard plastic cups. Wrap the top with plastic wrap and punch popsicle sticks through the plastic wrap. Freeze the containers until the smoothie is frozen solid.

All of the following recipes make one 18 to 20–ounce smoothie. All smoothies are at their peak when they are just made but if necessary they can sit in the fridge for one day.

THE SCOOP ON SUPERFOODS FOR YOUR SMOOTHIES

For an easy extra boost of veg-power you can add a handful of kale or spinach to any of the following smoothies except for the Chocolate Peanut Butter smoothie (why mess with perfection?).

But if you want to jazz up your smoothie health-wise even more, add superfoods. The following superfoods can be found in health food stores and online. Some of these powders and pulps can be expensive but a little goes along way and the benefits outweigh the price in my opinion. Just add a scoop or chunk to any of the following smoothies for added benefit.

ACAI BERRY PULP, FROZEN: Intense antioxidant, cancer fighter, and cholesterol control

ALOE VERA PULP, FRESH OR FROZEN: Anti-inflammatory, blood sugar stabilizer, and cholesterol control

CAMU POWDER: High in vitamin C and immunity-booster

CHIA SEEDS: Increase energy, anti-inflammatory, blood sugar stabilizer, and blood pressure reduction

GOJI BERRY POWDER OR DRIED BERRIES: Anti-aging, rich in protein, and immunity booster

HEMP SEEDS: Healthy skin, anti-inflammatory, and cholesterol control

MACA POWDER: Increase energy, improve mood, lower stress, high in vitamin B, and rich in protein

MAQUI POWDER: Antioxidant, anti-aging, and blood sugar stabilizer

MULBERRY FRUIT POWDER: Antioxidant, anti-inflammatory, and immunity booster

PROTEIN POWDER POWER

It's not absolutely necessary to consume protein powder just because you are vegan; however, it is a good idea at first, to ensure you are getting enough daily protein while you get your new diet in order. I add protein powder to my smoothies as a way of maximizing my workouts and as a quick meal replacement.

Finding the right protein powder can be exasperating. It's not cheap and it's not like you're going to be buying more soon because it's usually sold in giant containers. How to sort through all the noise? I recommend having a conversation with someone at your local health food store. Tell them what you're looking for and ask what their return policy is. Some places have very friendly return policies in terms of protein powder and, better yet, they may also have single-serving samples for you to try before you make a decision. Don't listen to anyone who tells you vegan protein powders are inferior to the animal-based ones; that is simply false and there are a lot of ripped vegan muscle-bound body builders and athletes to prove it.

Here's what you're looking for: 15 to 25g of protein with less than 10g carbohydrates and under 125 calories per serving. After that it's a matter of flavor. I recommend only buying vanilla-flavored or even plain protein powders; when you feel like jazzing it up it is easy to add a tablespoon of cocoa powder, a banana, a handful of berries, or a scoop of instant coffee. Lastly, be sure to read the list of ingredients if your tummy is sensitive to artificial sweeteners; some powders have a lot while others have none.

You can add a serving of plain or vanilla protein powder to any of the smoothie recipes below.

NOTE:

Here are the brands that I like; none of these companies pay me so it's just my honest opinion.

- Garden of Life RAW Protein
- Vegan proteins+
- Vega Sport Performance Protein
- Sunwarrior Classic Protein

(CONTINUED) >

chocolate and peanut butter

Simply put: Two great tastes that taste great together.

1 cup ice

1 banana

2 cups almond milk

2 tablespoons cocoa powder

2 tablespoons natural peanut butter (smooth is better)

1 Place all the ingredients in a blender pitcher and puree until smooth.

blueberry vanilla

Holy antioxidants, Batman! Blueberries are still the best common source of antioxidants and they are a wonderful balance of carbs and fiber, which makes them a great form of energy and good for your digestion. Get Blue!

2 cups frozen organic blueberries

1 cup almond milk

½ cup vanilla soy yogurt

1 Place all the ingredients in a blender pitcher and puree until smooth.

almond-melon heaven

It's truly amazing how delicious the flavors of almond and melon are together. Melons are a great source of vitamin B6 and niacin and they can be very filling, so this smoothie is the perfect portable breakfast (or snack) when your healthy choices are going to be limited.

½ cup raw almonds

1 cup almond milk

1½ cups chopped honeydew melon or cantaloupe

1 cup ice

1 Place all the ingredients in a blender pitcher and puree until the fruit is smooth and the almond chunks are still visible.

mango-kiwi baja style

I call these Baja style because as a kid I loved getting street fruit in Baja California, Mexico. The fruit was always served cold, on a stick, and covered with lime juice and chili powder. Really refreshing with a kick—just like this smoothie.

1 cup ice

1 cup frozen mango

1 cold kiwi, peeled and chopped

Juice of 1 lime

1 tablespoon coconut sugar (optional)

½ teaspoon chili powder

1 Place all the ingredients in a blender pitcher and puree until smooth.

cucumber-watermelon baja style

Like the mango-kiwi version, this has a sweet and spicy kick. Cucumber and watermelon are super light and great complements to each other.

1 cup ice

1½ cups cold watermelon, chopped

1½ cups cucumber, peeled, chopped

Juice of 1 lime

1 tablespoon coconut sugar (optional)

½ teaspoon chili powder

1 Place all the ingredients in a blender pitcher and puree until smooth.

mango peachiness

If you don't like mango and peaches together, check your pulse . . . you might be dead. If you have kids, this smoothie is particularly great for popsicles.

1 cup frozen mango

1 cup frozen peaches

1 cup vanilla soy yogurt

½ cup almond milk or more as needed to achieve desired texture

1 Place all the ingredients in a blender pitcher and puree until smooth.

strawberry-banana-almond

The almonds add protein, good fat, flavor, and crunch to this already yummy smoothie.

½ cup raw almonds

1 cup almond milk

1 medium banana

1 cup strawberries

1 pinch cinnamon

1 cup ice

1 Place all the ingredients in a blender pitcher and puree until the fruit is smooth and the almond chunks are still visible.

kiwi-strawberry-banana

This is a match made in fruit heaven. I love how banana makes any smoothie rich and creamy without adding a ton of calories. You could serve small glasses of this smoothie to your family as a summer dessert for sure. Any other fruit you have on hand would work seamlessly here, too.

2 cold kiwis, peeled and chopped

1 cup frozen strawberries

1 banana

1 cup almond milk

1 cup ice

1 Place all the ingredients in a blender pitcher and puree until smooth.

vanilla-raspberry-orange

You could call this smoothie a creamy raspberry Orange Julius. It's the perfect combination of orange and vanilla with all the fruity sweetness that comes from raspberries. My sons love this one.

1 cup frozen raspberries

Zest of 1 orange

1 cup orange juice

½ cup vanilla soy yogurt

½ teaspoon vanilla extract

1 Place all the ingredients in a blender pitcher and puree until smooth.

triple berry

Can't decide which antioxidant berry you love most? Have all three and go into a berry-induced coma. I have to admit that this smoothie is kind of begging for a healthy splash of rum.

½ cup frozen blackberries

½ cup frozen strawberries

½ cup frozen raspberries

1 cup almond milk

½ banana

1 Place all the ingredients in a blender pitcher and puree until smooth.

HIGH-FIBER BANANA BLUEBERRY MUFFINS

MAKES 3 DOZEN ROCKIN' MUFFINS

You want a great way to start the day? These muffins are IT. And, better yet—this recipe is super versatile: you can make the batter and bake the muffins right away, you can make and freeze the batter then defrost the batter and bake them fresh as often as you wish, or you can freeze the muffins when they are freshly baked and pop them in the oven to defrost and toast. Whatever you do, the end result is always yummy.

I like to see an even number of blueberries in each muffin so I add them by hand but if that's too OCD for you, you can just dump them all in the batter and then scoop away into the muffin cups.

2½ cups whole wheat flour

1½ cups oatmeal

1½ cups flaxseed meal

2 tablespoons baking powder

1 tablespoon ground cinnamon

½ cup organic white sugar

¾ cup organic brown sugar plus a small amount more for garnish

1½ cups applesauce

1 tablespoon vanilla extract

2.7 ounces (⅓ cup) melted vegan butter, grapeseed oil, or coconut oil

2½ cups almond milk

2 large organic bananas, peeled, cut in quarters lengthwise, and chopped thin, +1 large organic banana

Two 6-ounce cartons of fresh organic blueberries, or any other berry or chopped fresh fruit

1 Preheat the oven to 350°F. Prepare the muffin tins by rubbing the insides with a butter- or oil-dipped paper towel.

2 Using a stand mixer or a large bowl, mix the flour, oatmeal, flaxseed meal, baking powder, cinnamon, and sugars until they are fully combined. Mix in the applesauce, vanilla extract, butter, and almond milk until all the ingredients are well incorporated. Gently fold in the bananas. At this point the batter is complete and ready to be frozen or refrigerated.

3 Scoop the batter into the prepared muffin tins with a ¼-cup measuring cup or a ¼-cup ice-cream scoop. When all the muffin tins are full, distribute the blueberries evenly among the muffins then go back and for each push some of the blueberries down into the batter so they don't all sit at the top. Peel the third banana and slice it as thin as possible. Place 2 to 3 slices of banana on each muffin then sprinkle the tops with just a pinch of brown sugar.

4 Bake the muffins for 20 to 25 minutes or until a toothpick comes out clean.

5 If freezing baked muffins, wait until they are completely cool then bag them or freeze them inside a plastic container with a tight-fitting lid. If you choose to freeze the batter; place it in a resealable plastic bag and lay it flat and thin rather than in a large block—this makes defrosting quick and easy.

BAKED MUFFINS ARE GOOD FOR 3 DAYS COVERED AND UNREFRIGERATED.

BEST OAT-FREE OATMEAL EVER

MAKES 4 SERVINGS

I once had a client who ate oatmeal every morning. Every. Morning. So I decided to shake it up a bit and whipped this recipe up. I wanted to deliver on the request while also making something different than plain old oatmeal. The final result? Hearty, with protein and fiber and enough sweetness to make it all taste great. My client was *very* pleased and so was I. And here's the funny part: it wasn't until later that I realized there are actually no oats in this recipe!

Maqui berry powder is exceptionally good for you; it's high in antioxidants and acts as an anti-inflammatory, which aids in digestion and circulation. I like to add it inconspicuously to any breakfast item. You can find it in natural grocery stores or online.

2 cups farro

½ cup chia seeds

2½ cups almond milk, rice milk, or soy milk

1 tablespoon vanilla powder or vanilla extract

1 tablespoon maqui powder

1 tablespoon cinnamon

2 tablespoons agave syrup

2 tablespoons maple syrup

½ cup sliced almonds

1 cup fresh plums or strawberries, chopped small

½ cup dried apricots, chopped small

1 Rinse and drain the farro. Place it in a medium-size saucepan with 5 cups of water. Bring the water to a boil; reduce heat to medium-low and simmer 30 minutes or until tender. Drain any excess water and discard.

2 Place the farro, chia seeds, milk, vanilla powder, maqui powder, cinnamon, and syrups in a 3 to 4–quart saucepan over medium heat and bring it to a simmer. Stir until the cereal begins to thicken slightly, about 3 minutes.

3 Remove the cereal from the heat and add the almonds and fruit. Divide the oatmeal evenly into four medium-size bowls and serve immediately.

ALTHOUGH IT'S BEST WHEN FRESH, OATMEAL IS GOOD FOR 2 DAYS REFRIGERATED. REHEAT WITH A DASH OF MILK.

OATMEAL CRUNCH GRANOLA

MAKES 5 CUPS

Granola is one of my favorite things to have on hand, but let's face it, really good-quality granola can get pricey. I never knew how easy and better it was to make my own until I tried it. Here is a basic recipe that is great on its own but is also super versatile. You can add to it your favorite ingredients like sliced almonds, coconut, cinnamon, seeds of any kind, and dried fruit. While you can add nuts, seeds, or spices to the mix before baking, the dried fruit should be added when the granola is done but still warm.

4 cups old-fashioned oatmeal or rolled oats

1 cup pecan pieces

1 pinch kosher salt

3 tablespoons grapeseed or safflower oil

½ cup maple syrup

¾ cup brown sugar

1 Preheat the oven to 325°F. Add all the ingredients to a large bowl and mix until well combined.

2 Spread the mixture out onto two sheet trays or two large glass casserole dishes. (I like to use the casserole dishes because it is easier to mix the hot cereal without spilling.)

3 Bake the granola for 1 hour and 15 minutes, stirring every 15 minutes to achieve an even color.

4 Allow the granola to cool completely then break up any large pieces that might be stuck together.

STORE THE GRANOLA IN AN AIRTIGHT CONTAINER; IT WILL KEEP FOR AT LEAST 1 MONTH.

CRISP, FLAKY, BAD BOYS;
aka VEGAN CROISSANTS

MAKES 22 TO 24 CROISSANTS

I know, who wants to make their own croissants? They can seem like a tough thing to pull off but they really aren't that hard. The key is jump right in, tackle the recipe, and get your first batch under your belt and you'll be a pro.

Traditional croissants involve laminating the dough with a layer of butter in the middle then rolling it out and folding it and repeating the process a gazillion times. While my method requires a little bit of that process, it is ultimately much easier because the butter is already mixed in the dough.

The dough will need to rest a day before you can bake these guys and eat them up, but come to terms with that little detail and I promise it will be worth the wait.

---

2 cups all-purpose flour

2 cups bread flour

¼ cup organic coconut sugar

1½ teaspoons kosher salt

1 tablespoon active dry yeast (not Rapid-Rise), about 1½ little ¼-ounce envelopes

4 ounces (½ cup) solidified coconut oil

8 ounces (1 cup) vegan butter, cut into small cubes

1⅓ cups cold almond milk

PREPARE THE DOUGH

1 In a large bowl mix the flours, sugar, salt, and yeast. Set aside.

2 Using a small spoon, dollop the coconut oil onto a plate and place it in the freezer with the cubed butter for 15 minutes. (The butter cubes should be twice the size of the coconut oil dollops).

3 Place about 2½ cups of the flour mixture in a food processor and add the frozen butter and oil. Pulse about five times until the chunks are slightly larger than pea size. Add the contents of the food processor to the rest of the flour then fold in the almond milk with a rubber spatula or wooden spoon until a dough forms. (Do not over mix or the butter will melt.) Wrap the bowl well with plastic wrap and refrigerate it overnight and up to 48 hours.

ROLL THE CROISSANTS

1 Remove the dough from the refrigerator. Plop the sticky dough onto a well-floured flat surface. Dust the dough with flour generously and roll it into a large rectangle somewhere around 10 x 30 inches, dusting often to prevent the dough from sticking to the surface or rolling pin.

(CONTINUED) >

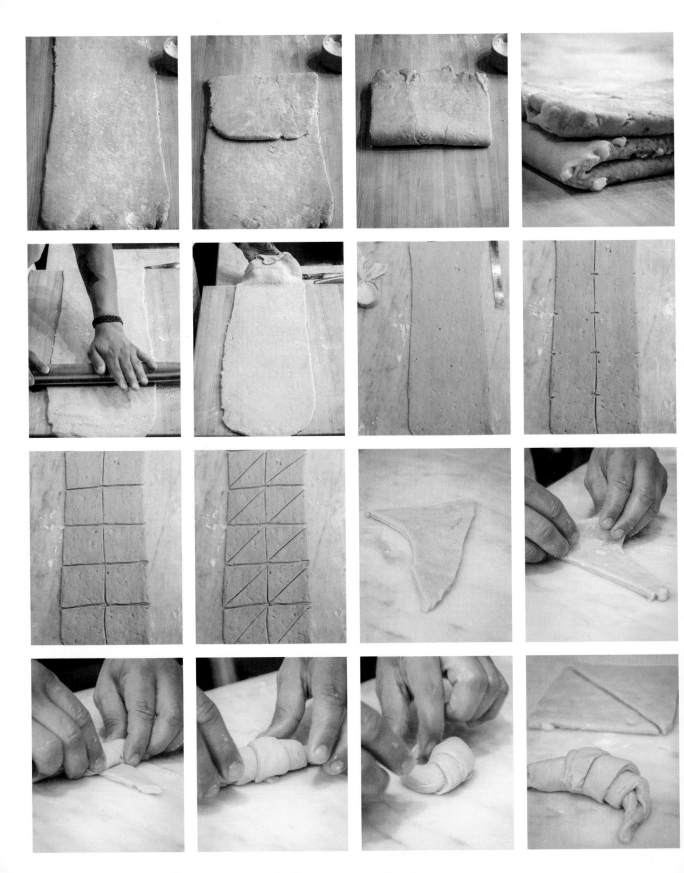

2 Fold the dough in thirds by folding the short end up and past the midpoint of the dough then fold the opposite side up over the top like a business letter. Give the dough a quarter turn and roll it out again into about a 10 x 30-inch rectangle. Fold the dough in thirds again then cover it and let it rest 15 to 30 minutes in the fridge.

3 While the dough is in the fridge line two 13 x 18-inch baking sheets with parchment paper.

4 Remove the dough from the fridge and roll it out one last time into an exact 10 x 30-inch rectangle. Trim away any excess dough and save it to make an extra croissant or two.

5 Using a ruler, mark both long sides of the dough every 5 inches with a paring knife. Mark the short side in half, and using a knife or pizza cutter, cut the dough in half lengthwise. You should now have two 5 x 30-inch strips of dough. Using a ruler, score both newly cut long sides of the dough every 5 inches. Now cut the dough into triangles by starting at one corner and following your cut marks. You should have twenty-two triangles in all.

6 Gently stretch the base of each triangle then pull the tip of the triangle to make it less of a right triangle and more like an isosceles triangle. (It should look like a slice of pizza). Dust off as much flour from the triangle as possible. Secure the tip to the counter with an object or your finger while gently pulling the base toward yourself as you roll the croissant from the base to the tip.

7 Place each croissant on the baking sheet with the tips of the triangle tucked underneath. Pull the croissant ends and pull them inward to create the crescent shape.

PROOF AND BAKE

1 Loosely cover the croissants with plastic wrap and let them rise at room temperature for 2½ hours; after 2 hours preheat the oven to 350°F.

2 Bake the croissants for about 30 minutes, stopping halfway through the baking process to rotate the trays and switch their positions.

3 Let the croissants rest 30 minutes (if you can) before eating. You can freeze the freshly baked croissants as soon as they are completely cool. The best way to defrost the croissants is to let them sit out until they are room temp then bake or toast them until crisp.

3

MAKE YOUR LUNCH BREAK

LOW-CARB RAW TACO WRAPS

MAKES 8 WRAPS

The secret here is using a hearty lettuce leaf instead of a tortilla. Taco sacrilege? Well, the "meat" here is almonds and walnuts—for a flavor and texture that is out of this world and so good, you won't miss the shell!

Of course, you can also enjoy these with corn or flour tortillas, but they would no longer be "low-carb."

1½ cups raw walnuts, rinsed in hot water

1½ cups raw blanched almonds, rinsed in hot water

1 tablespoon + 1 teaspoon ground cumin

1 teaspoon chili powder

1 teaspoon garlic powder

1 teaspoon onion powder

½ bunch cilantro, stems included, finely chopped

3 firm plum tomatoes, quartered lengthwise, hearts removed, diced very small

Kosher salt and freshly ground black pepper to taste

1 head butter lettuce for the wrap

½ firm avocado

Chipotle Nut Cream for serving (page 18)

1 Place the walnuts and almonds in a food processor and add all the dry spices. Pulse the nuts in 2-second intervals until they look coarsely ground or minced. Do not overgrind!

2 Place the ground nuts in a medium bowl; add the cilantro and tomato. Mix until combined. Season well with salt and pepper. Be sure the mixture is room temperature, not cold.

3 Remove the leaves from the head of lettuce and pick eight good, intact leaves to use for the tacos. Wash and pat dry.

4 Scoop out the avocado flesh and slice it into eight equal-size wedges. Spoon ⅛ of the nut mixture into a lettuce leaf and top it with an avocado wedge then drizzle the taco generously with chipotle cream.

TACOS *de* PAPA *con* CHORIZO

MAKES 12 TACOS

The secret to these bad boys is the homemade tofu-rizo. Mixed with potatoes and lightly seasoned, you'll have a protein-packed meal that's great with any of the salsas in the basics chapter. And of course, guacamole.

4 russet potatoes, peeled and cut into ½-inch chunks

2 tablespoons extra-virgin olive oil

1 batch Roberto's Tofu-Rizo (page 10) or one 12-ounce package Soyrizo

2 teaspoons dried oregano

Eighteen 6-inch corn tortillas

1 batch Basic Guacamole (page 27)

1 batch Salsa Mojada (page 31)

¼ large green cabbage, shredded thin

1 Cook the potatoes in a large saucepan of boiling salted water until they are just cooked through but still hold their shape, about 5 to 7 minutes. Drain the liquid and return the potatoes to the pot. Heat the potatoes in the dry pot over medium heat for 2 minutes to dry them out.

2 Heat a large skillet over medium heat then add the olive oil and wait for it to shimmer. Add the potatoes to the pan and brown them slightly, about 15 minutes, then add the tofu-rizo and oregano and stir for 3 to 5 minutes. Give the potatoes a gentle smash to incorporate with the tofu-rizo, then remove the pan from the heat and cover to keep the filling warm.

3 Heat a nonstick skillet or cast-iron pan over high heat until it is very hot. Cook the corn tortillas in the hot dry pan for about 2 minutes per side. (A few toasted/burn marks are desired.)

4 Fill the tortillas with a few spoonfuls of the potato mixture then some guacamole, some salsa, and a few pinches of shredded cabbage. Serve with your favorite hot sauce on the side.

5 Refrigerate any leftover taco filling in an airtight container. Filling is good for 3 days.

BLACK BEAN MUSHROOM BURGERS

MAKES 8 BURGERS

My nine-year-old son claims he *hates* mushrooms . . . but he loves these burgers. The secret? Black beans mixed with mushrooms and farro for a meaty texture—without all the additives and junk that's in some packaged veggie burgers. These family-friendly patties can be made two days ahead and stored in the fridge or freezer until ready to use. Better yet, cook up a double batch and freeze half for a quick lunch or dinner later.

1 teaspoon extra-virgin olive oil

1 medium white onion, diced small

1 pound button or Cremini mushrooms, chopped small

1 cup dried black beans cooked until very tender and strained from the cooking liquid (see method on page 84) or two 15-ounce cans black beans, drained and rinsed

1 cup farro simmered in 3 cups water until tender and drained

1 tablespoon garlic powder

2 tablespoons reduced-sodium soy sauce

A few dashes hot sauce (I like El Tapatio and Chalula)

1 teaspoon liquid smoke

Kosher salt and freshly ground black pepper to taste

2 tablespoons high-heat oil, like grapeseed or safflower

1 Heat a sauté pan or skillet over high heat. Add the oil and wait until it shimmers, about 30 seconds.

2 Add the onions and stir with a wooden spoon until the onions turn golden brown, about 8 minutes. Add the mushrooms and sauté 5 minutes more or until the pan is nearly dry. Remove the pan from the heat and allow the onion mixture to cool.

3 Place the beans and half the farro in a food processor with the garlic powder, soy sauce, hot sauce, and liquid smoke and pulse until well combined. Scoop the bean and farro mixture into a large bowl. Stir in the onions mixture and the remaining farro. Taste the mixture and season accordingly.

4 Scoop a half-cup of the bean mixture and shape it into a patty and set aside. Repeat until all the mixture is used.

NOTE:

If you want to grill the veggie burgers, cook them first as instructed above and allow them to cool on a sheet tray then grill them until warm inside, about 2 minutes per side. Cooking them in a pan dries them out a little bit and forms a crust, which will allow them to stay together on the grill.

5 Heat a skillet and add 1 tablespoon high-heat oil, place four patties in the skillet, and cook over medium-high heat for about 2 minutes per side. Use a strong metal spatula to gently flip the patties. Transfer the patties to a sheet tray or large plate. Add the remaining tablespoon of oil to the pan and cook the remaining 4 patties in the same fashion.

6 Serve warm with standard hamburger fixings or serve them as is over grilled asparagus or roasted broccoli. (See pages 36 for mayo, 38 for ketchup, and 21 for pickles.)

EASY BEAN SOAKING AND COOKING, TWO WAYS

Beans are a crucial protein source in the life of a vegan, so learning to prepare them properly is imperative. Canned beans are great: they are quick, easy, and perfect if you find yourself in a pinch. But dried beans taste better, they don't have to contain sodium, as many canned beans do, and they are cheaper—not to mention kinder to the environment.

In order to make beans digestible, they need to be soaked before cooking. There are two widely accepted ways of doing this. I'm not partial to any particular method; they are both fine. One requires the beans to soak overnight; the other is a quick-soak method, but it requires longer cooking time. So for you, it's just a matter of planning.

When it comes to cooking beans there are a few basics to remember:

Choose what method you plan to use to soak the beans.

Use a heavy-bottom stockpot to reduce the chances of scorching the beans on the bottom.

Use plenty of water and cover the beans, especially if you plan to leave them cooking unattended. Burnt beans are a waste and they can stink up a house worse than anything.

Only use aromatics while cooking the beans; things like herbs, garlic, onions, and pepper are great but salt in any form toughens the beans and slows down the cooking process. Beans do require salt for flavor but only add it when the beans are soft. If a recipe calls for cooking the beans in a broth or sauce expect the cooking time to increase.

METHOD 1: OVERNIGHT
(1 CUP DRY BEANS TO 5 CUPS WATER)

Rinse the beans and place them in a large bowl or container with five times as much room-temperature water as beans. Let the beans soak covered overnight. (It's okay to refrigerate the beans but it is not necessary.) After the beans have soaked a minimum of 8 hours, drain and rinse them, discarding the soaking liquid. You may then store the soaked beans for 2 days in the fridge or cook them in water until soft. Do not season the beans until they are fully cooked. Cooking time depends greatly on the type and quantity of beans but 45 minutes to 1 hour at a constant simmer is the average.

METHOD 2: THE QUICK-SOAK

This method reduces the soaking time but extends the cooking time. Rinse the beans and place them in a pot with five times the amount of water. Bring the beans to a simmer for 5 minutes, then remove them from the heat and allow the beans to soak for at least 1 hour. Drain and rinse the beans, discarding the soaking liquid. Beans that have been quick-soaked should be cooked that same day. Cook the beans with plenty of water until soft. Do not season the beans until they are fully cooked. Cooking time depends greatly on the type and quantity of beans but 1½ hours at a constant simmer is the average.

NOTES

½ cup dry beans will yield the equivalent of one 14-ounce can of beans.

BAD BOY PULLED BARBECUE SANDWICHES

MAKES 4 SANDWICHES

Let's face it: the success of any sandwich relies heavily on the quality of the bun. When I make a sandwich at home it is usually because I have come across some perfect bread that begs for a higher purpose. People put too much focus on the sandwich filling and pick up whatever bread is available. To that I say "Negatory, amigo! Let the bun lead the way." If you adopt this mantra I promise your sandwich life will improve. When the universe decides to put the perfect bun in your hands run home and make these bad boy sandwiches. (Of course, the filling here is pretty awesome. You never thought that cabbage and celeriac would make a killer vehicle for BBQ sauce? Well think again.)

1 large Napa cabbage

2 celeriac bulbs

1 bunch scallions, green parts only, cut on the bias

1 bunch cilantro, stems included, chopped

1 batch Bourbon BBQ Sauce (page 46)

4 awesome sandwich buns

1 firm avocado

1 Slice the cabbage crosswise into thin strips (about 1/16 inch thick). Cut the celeriac into similar size matchsticks or grate (see note).

2 In a large soup or stockpot toss the cabbage, celeriac, scallions, and cilantro with enough barbecue sauce to coat the vegetables generously. Place the pot over medium heat and stir until the mixture is warm and wilted (about 5 to 10 minutes only).

3 Toast four buns to perfection. Place a heaping mound of the warm pulled barbecue slaw on half a bun. Top the slaw with 1/4 sliced avocado.

4 Serve with your favorite salad, my Celeriac Salad (page 129), or Perfectly Baked Yam Fries (page 150) and Bread and Butter Pickles (page 24).

THE PULLED VEGGIE BBQ FILLING WILL LAST 4 DAYS REFRIGERATED.

NOTE:

The recipe calls for the celeriac sliced into thin strips. If this is pretty much impossible for you, rather than chopping it up all chunky, grate the celeriac on the large side of a box grater.

"LOBSTER" QUICHE *(Soy Free)*

MAKES 6 SERVINGS

I love tofu but I know some folks are sensitive to soy and some of us who have been vegan for a while get a bit tofu-ed out. If you are in the mood for something REALLY different, bust out this quiche and you will not be disappointed. The chickpea flour binds everything together the way eggs would. Turmeric provides flavor and color and the Himalayan salt has a natural subtle sulfur flavor that, when combined with the other ingredients, really resembles egg flavor. Here's the crazy part . . . between the turmeric, cauliflower, and yeast an unusual flavor develops that truly resembles fresh lobster! This quiche is astoundingly delicious.

½ batch Perfect Pie Dough (page 233)

4 tablespoons extra-virgin olive oil

1 small white onion, diced small

1 red bell pepper, diced small

1 zucchini, dice small

2 cups cauliflower, chopped into small florets

3 garlic cloves, minced

1 pound button mushrooms, sliced thin

Kosher salt and freshly ground black pepper to taste

1½ cups chickpea flour

1 teaspoon baking powder

½ teaspoon turmeric

¼ cup nutritional yeast

1 teaspoon Himalayan pink salt

1½ cups Better than Bouillon "No Chicken" Chicken Broth or Rich Yellow Vegetable Stock (page 116)

FOR THE CRUST

1 Preheat the oven to 375°F.

2 Roll out the dough large enough to cover a 9 to 10–inch pie pan or a tart pan. Poke little holes all over the crust to prevent air bubbles. Cover the crust with parchment paper and fill the dish with pie weights or dried beans. Bake the crust for about 12 minutes or until crisp and allow the crust to cool.

3 Carefully remove the pie weights. If using dried beans, save the beans and label them to use again for the same purpose.

FOR THE FILLING

1 Reduce the oven to 350°F.

2 Heat a large skillet or sauté pan over high heat. Sprinkle the dry pan with salt then add 2 tablespoons of the olive oil and wait for it to shimmer, about 30 seconds.

3 Add the onions and bell pepper and stir until the onions are golden brown (about 12 minutes). Add the zucchini and cauliflower and stir for about 5 minutes. Add the garlic and cook for just 2 minutes more, then place veggies in medium bowl and set aside. Wipe the pan with a paper towel and return it to the heat.

4 Add remaining 2 tablespoons of olive oil and wait for it to shimmer. Add the sliced mushrooms and cook them until the liquid they release has evaporated and the 'shrooms are brown, about 12 minutes. Season the mushrooms with salt and pepper then add them to the other vegetables. Set aside.

5 Place the chickpea flour in a large bowl with the baking powder, turmeric, nutritional yeast, and Himalayan pink salt. Whisk in the broth until a thick batter is formed. Mix in the vegetables until they are well coated in the batter. Pour the quiche batter into the prepared piecrust and bake for 40 to 50 minutes or until brown and set. Allow the quiche to rest for 15 minutes before slicing.

LEFTOVER QUICHE IS GOOD COVERED AND STORED IN THE REFRIGERATOR FOR 3 DAYS.

SPINACH *and* SUNDRIED TOMATO QUICHE

MAKES 6 SERVINGS

Quiche is the best thing to serve at a brunch because it straddles breakfast and lunch perfectly. It's good warm or room temperature so you don't have to babysit it. The extra cool thing about an egg-free quiche is that you can taste it before you bake it so there is no excuse for it to be underseasoned.

½ batch Perfect Pie Dough (page 233)

One 14-ounce block organic firm tofu

2 tablespoons extra-virgin olive oil

1 medium white onion, diced small

1 yellow bell pepper, seeded, diced small

10 ounces organic baby spinach

2 garlic cloves, minced

½ bunch scallions, green parts only, sliced very thin

10 big basil leaves, chopped

3 ounces sun-dried tomatoes, chopped

2 tablespoons nutritional yeast

½+ teaspoon Himalayan pink salt to taste (kosher salt can be substituted here, but Himalayan pink salt adds a distinct "egg" flavor to the final product)

Freshly ground black pepper to taste

FOR THE CRUST

1 Preheat the oven to 375°F.

2 Roll out the dough large enough to cover a 9 to 10–inch pie pan or a tart pan. Poke little holes all over the crust to prevent air bubbles. Cover the crust with parchment paper and fill the dish with pie weights or dried beans. Bake the crust for about 12 minutes or until crisp and allow the crust to cool.

3 Carefully remove the pie weights. If using dried beans save the beans and label them to use again for the same purpose.

FOR THE FILLING

1 First, press your tofu. Cut the tofu into eight equal pieces lengthwise and lay them flat on a paper towel–lined kitchen towel. Cover the tofu with paper towels then place an additional kitchen towel over the tofu. Press down hard on the tofu to remove as much water as possible. (It's OK if the tofu bursts or crumbles a bit . . . keep squeezing.)

2 Place the pressed tofu in the bowl of a food processor fitted with the S blade. Puree the tofu until smooth then set it aside.

3 Heat a large skillet or sauté pan over high heat. Add the olive oil and wait for it to shimmer. Add the onion and cook until golden brown (about 10 minutes). Add the bell pepper and cook until soft (about 4 minutes). Add the spinach to the pan, stir and cover the spinach then remove the pan from the heat to allow the spinach to wilt (2 to 3 minutes).

When the spinach is wilted remove the lid and return the pan to the heat. Cook the mixture until all the spinach water has evaporated, about 4 minutes.

4 Place the spinach mixture in a medium bowl and add the garlic, scallions, basil, tomatoes, and nutritional yeast. Stir in the smooth tofu and season aggressively with salt and pepper. Mix the ingredients really well and spoon the filling into the crust.

5 Bake the quiche for about 20 minutes or less depending on its thickness. Carefully reach in the oven and using an oven mitt or tongs shake the quiche a bit. When the filling is no longer wobbly the quiche is done. In this case underdone is better than burnt. This quiche is very forgiving and will set up nicely after it rests. Allow the quiche to rest for 15 minutes before slicing. Cover and refrigerate.

LEFTOVER QUICHE IS GOOD COVERED AND STORED IN THE REFRIGERATOR FOR 3 DAYS.

4 | I'VE GOT BIG BOWLS

CLASSIC POTATO SOUP

MAKES 6 SERVINGS

Sometimes I think people forget what a difference fresh herbs can make in a simple dish. Rosemary and potatoes always go great together, even in a soup, but the basil and chives added at the end take this potato soup to the next level of bliss. You'll want to cozy up to a warm bowl of this soup and forget the chaotic world around you . . . at least for 10 minutes. It's too good to keep to yourself, so surprise a friend by dropping off some of this soup to remind them you care. I guarantee it will make their day.

2 tablespoons extra-virgin olive oil

1 large white onion, diced small

4 ribs celery, diced small

2 teaspoons fresh rosemary, minced

4 garlic cloves, minced

2 fat carrots, diced small

8 cups Better than Bouillon "No Beef" Beef Broth or Rich Dark Vegetable Stock (page 117)

¼ cup all-purpose flour

1½ cups almond milk

5 medium yellow potatoes, scrubbed clean and diced medium with skins on

1 tablespoon liquid smoke

10 large fresh basil leaves, chopped

2 tablespoons finely chopped chives

Kosher salt and freshly ground black pepper to taste

1 Heat a large stockpot over medium-high heat. Add the olive oil and wait until it shimmers then add the onions and celery and stir with a wooden spoon until they are translucent, about 5 minutes. Add the rosemary, garlic, and carrots and stir for a minute then add the broth and bring it to a simmer then remove it from the heat.

2 Place the flour in a medium bowl and whisk in the almond milk to create a batter. Whisk about 2 cups of the broth from the soup pot into the flour mixture until completely blended then add the flour mixture into the soup.

3 Place the soup over high heat and stir until it comes to a boil, then adjust the heat to maintain a constant but gentle simmer. Simmer the soup for 10 minutes, scraping the bottom occasionally with a wooden spoon to prevent scorching.

4 Add the potatoes and simmer until they are tender, about 15 minutes. When the potatoes are fully cooked stir in the liquid smoke and herbs and season with salt and pepper.

5 Ladle about 1½ cups into deep bowls and serve immediately.

THE SOUP IS GOOD FOR 5 DAYS IN THE FRIDGE. SURPRISINGLY, THIS SOUP FREEZES VERY WELL, JUST BE SURE TO FREEZE IT FLAT IN A BAG TO MAKE DEFROSTING QUICK AND EASY. IT'LL LAST TWO MONTHS FROZEN.

CREAMY *and* SMOKY TOMATO SOUP

MAKES 6 SERVINGS

What makes *this* tomato soup better than the rest? Cashews! The cashews create that rich creaminess usually provided by copious amounts of heavy cream. The "smoky" is courtesy of a handy ingredient called liquid smoke—a little goes a long way. This soup is not only delicious and comforting but it is totally easy.

2 tablespoons extra-virgin olive oil

2 medium yellow onions, diced small

4 garlic cloves, minced

8 large vine-ripened tomatoes, use the easy-peel method (page 40) then coarsely chop, reserving as much juice as possible

5 cups Better than Bouillon "No Chicken" Chicken Broth or Rich Yellow Vegetable Stock (page 116)

1 cup raw cashews

1 teaspoon liquid smoke

10 fresh basil leaves, chopped

Kosher salt and freshly ground black pepper to taste

TIP:

When blending hot liquids always use the lid but remove the little fill cap and cover the hole with a folded kitchen towel. The idea is to allow air to escape from the pitcher and prevent the hot liquid from jumping out of the pitcher and causing harm. ("The more you know . . .")

1 Heat a small stockpot over high heat. Add the olive oil and wait until it shimmers then add the onions and stir with a wooden spoon until the onions are golden brown (about 12 minutes). Add the garlic and continue stirring for one minute more. Add the chopped tomatoes and all of the tomato juice. Stir and continue cooking over high heat for about 2 minutes to concentrate the flavors then gently pour in the broth. Reduce the heat to medium-low and simmer the soup for 5 minutes then remove the soup from the heat.

2 In a small saucepan simmer the cashews with 4 cups of water for 5 minutes. Drain and rinse the cashews. Place the cooked cashews in a blender pitcher with the liquid smoke and half of the soup.

3 Carefully puree the hot soup until the mixture is completely smooth. Stir the pureed mixture back into the soup and bring it to a gentle simmer. Allow the soup to simmer gently for about 10 minutes, stirring occasionally.

4 Stir in the basil and season the soup to taste with salt and pepper. Serve immediately. Allow any remaining soup to cool completely before storing in an airtight container and refrigerating.

SOUP IS GOOD FOR 5 DAYS REFRIGERATED OR 2 MONTHS FROZEN.

ROASTED RED BELL PEPPER SOUP

MAKES 6 SERVINGS

Hands down my favorite scent in the kitchen is the wafting bouquet of peppers roasting over an open flame. It's a perfect balance of sugar, chile, and char that I find intoxicating. Don't bother turning the exhaust fan on . . . let the whole house know you are doing some serious cooking and trust that this soup will deliver on the promises made by its aroma.

For a satisfying lunch or dinner I recommend serving this soup with my Curried Chickpea Salad (page 130) or the Herbaceous and Nutty Wheat Berry Salad (page 127).

6 red bell peppers

2 tablespoons high-heat oil, like grapeseed or safflower

2 medium white onions, chopped

½ teaspoon chili powder

2 large fat carrots, peeled and chopped

6 garlic cloves, crushed

6 cups Better than Bouillon "No Chicken" Chicken Broth or Rich Yellow Vegetable Stock (page 116)

1 small russet potato, peeled and quartered

Kosher salt and freshly ground black pepper to taste

½ bunch fresh cilantro, stems included, chopped

1 Wash and dry the peppers well then place them directly over a high flame, two peppers per burner. (If you don't have a gas stove, see broiler instructions in the note below.) Turn the peppers with a pair of metal tongs to char all sides. When all surfaces of the peppers are black, place the peppers in a large bowl and cover the bowl to steam the skins.

2 Rub the black skin off the peppers with a paper towel. If you didn't use the broiler remove the seeds but try to save any liquid that has accumulated in the pepper. Roughly chop the skinned peppers and place them in a bowl and set them aside.

3 Heat a large soup pot or small stockpot over high heat. Add the oil and wait for it to shimmer. Add the onions, chili powder, carrots, and garlic. Cook and stir until the vegetables are golden brown and show small signs of charring, about 12 minutes. Add the broth, peppers, and potato and bring the soup to a boil. Reduce the heat to low and allow the soup to simmer gently until the potato is very tender.

NOTE:

To roast peppers using your broiler, cut the peppers in half lengthwise and remove the seeds and membrane. Preheat the broiler and place the peppers cut side down on a sheet tray. Broil the peppers until the skins turn black and blistered. Place the peppers in a large bowl and cover the bowl to steam the skins. Proceed with the instructions as noted.

4 Remove the soup from the heat and allow it to cool slightly. Carefully puree the soup in a blender until it is smooth. Season the soup with salt and pepper. Garnish the soup with chopped cilantro and serve.

THE SOUP IS GOOD FOR 5 DAYS IN THE FRIDGE AND 2 MONTHS FROZEN.

TIP

When blending hot liquids always use the lid but remove the little fill cap and cover the hole with a folded kitchen towel. The idea is to allow air to escape from the pitcher and prevent the hot liquid from jumping out of the pitcher and causing harm. ("The more you know . . .")

SIMPLE RED LENTIL SOUP

MAKES 4 SERVINGS

I call them red lentils, others label them orange lentils, but trust me, they are the same. What matters is that these are the perfect soup lentils. They get tender fast and are very flavorful. I recommend keeping the lentils and broth separate until the last minute, otherwise the lentils will soak up all the liquid and your soup will turn into a pot of mush.

10 ounces (about 1½ cups) red lentils, rinsed

3+ cups water

Kosher salt and freshly ground black pepper to taste

1 tablespoon extra-virgin olive oil

1 large onion, diced small

3 garlic cloves, minced

6 cups Better than Bouillon "No Chicken" Chicken Broth or Rich Yellow Vegetable Stock (page 116)

2 medium carrots, peeled and diced really small

1 teaspoon fresh thyme leaves, chopped

1 teaspoon ground cumin

1 In a large saucepan combine the lentils with 3 cups cool water. Do not season the lentils. Bring the lentils to a simmer over high heat then reduce the heat to maintain a very gentle simmer. Cook the lentils uncovered for about 20 minutes or until they are just tender. Periodically add just enough water to keep the lentils barely covered.

2 When the lentils are fully cooked remove them from the heat, season them with salt and pepper then cover and set them aside. While the lentils are cooking start the soup.

3 Heat a 4-quart saucepan or small stockpot over medium-high heat. Add the olive oil and wait until it shimmers then add the onions and stir with a wooden spoon until the onions are slightly brown, about 8 minutes. Add the garlic and stir 1 minute more.

4 Carefully pour in the broth then add the carrots, thyme, and cumin. Simmer the soup only 2 to 3 minutes more. Remove the pot from the heat and cover the broth until ready to assemble and serve.

5 To assemble, bring the broth to a gentle simmer. Scoop 4 heaping spoonfuls of lentils into a medium bowl and ladle just over a cup of hot broth over the lentils then give the soup a gentle stir. Serve immediately.

THE SOUP AND COOKED LENTILS ARE GOOD FOR 5 DAYS REFRIGERATED. THE BROTH IS GOOD FOR 2 MONTHS FROZEN. I SUPPOSE YOU COULD FREEZE THE LENTILS, TOO, BUT I'VE NEVER DONE IT. I WOULD EAT THE LEFTOVER LENTILS IN A SALAD AND COOK A NEW BATCH WHEN YOU DECIDE TO DEFROST THE BROTH.

WILD MUSHROOM SOUP

I'm crazy about mushrooms. If you're not, this one may just convert you—this soup is a total winner. There are all kinds of wild mushrooms out there, but they can get pretty pricey; since their individual nuances get lost in soup, I keep the body of the soup inexpensive by using button or cremini mushrooms. The secret to the big wild mushroom flavor is the small amount of dried porcinis, which are unbelievably fragrant and intense. The potato and cashews give the soup its characteristic creamy richness. I highly recommend you make a double batch when making this soup because it acts as the sauce in my Grilled Vegetable Lasagne with Wild Mushroom Sauce (page 165). Having a batch in the freezer makes the lasagne preparation much less laborious.

2 ounces dried porcini mushrooms

½ cup raw cashews

1½ cups almond milk

2 tablespoons extra-virgin olive oil

2 to 3 fat leeks, white and pale green parts, halved lengthwise then rinsed well and sliced thin

4 garlic cloves, crushed

1 pound (16 ounces) button or cremini mushrooms, washed and patted dry, then chopped (presliced are OK)

1 cup cream sherry (I like *Harvey's Bristol Cream Sherry*, but any will do)

6 cups Better than Bouillon "No Chicken" Chicken Broth or Rich Yellow Vegetable Stock (page 117)

1 large russet potato, peeled and cubed

Kosher salt and freshly ground black pepper

2 tablespoons chopped chives

1 Quickly rinse the dried porcini mushrooms in very cold water for just a second or two.

2 Bring 2½ cups of water to a simmer in a small saucepan and remove it from the heat. Add the dried mushrooms and steep them for 20 minutes. Drain the mushrooms, reserving the soaking liquid. Allow the liquid to sit undisturbed for about 10 minutes to allow any grit and sediment to sink to the bottom. (I like to use a tall, narrow glass or measuring pitcher for this process.) Roughly chop the mushrooms and set them aside.

3 In a small saucepan bring the cashews to a boil in 2 cups water. Turn off the heat and soak them for about 30 minutes. Drain the cashews and discard the soaking liquid. Using a blender, puree the cashews in the almond milk until smooth and set it aside.

4 Heat a medium soup pot over high heat, add the olive oil, and wait for it to shimmer. Carefully add the leeks, as they may be slightly wet. Stir the leeks with a wooden spoon until they are wilted, about 4 minutes. Add the garlic and cook for 1 minute more then add the button mushrooms and sauté until they release their juices and start to brown, about 8 minutes. Stir in the porcini mushrooms and add the sherry and bring it to a simmer for about 5 minutes to intensify the flavors and cook out the alcohol.

5 Gently pour in the top three-quarters of the mushroom water and discard the rest. Allow the liquid to reduce by half, then stir in the broth and add the chopped potato. Bring the soup to a gentle simmer and reduce the heat.

6 Simmer the soup until the potato pieces are very tender, about 12 minutes, then add the cashew/almond cream, stirring to fully mix. Season the soup generously with salt and pepper and remove it from the heat. At this point you may choose to chop the soup with an emersion blender and serve it chunky or place the soup in a blender and puree it until smooth. Serve with chopped chives.

SOUP IS GOOD FOR 3 TO 4 DAYS REFRIGERATED OR UP TO 3 MONTHS FROZEN.

TIP

When blending hot liquids always use the lid but remove the little fill cap and cover the hole with a folded kitchen towel. The idea is to allow air to escape from the pitcher and prevent the hot liquid from jumping out of the pitcher and causing harm. ("The more you know . . .")

PUMPKIN CURRY SOUP *with* BASIL OIL *and* TOASTED HAZELNUTS

MAKES 6 SERVINGS

Pumpkin and curry is a match made in heaven. The rich silkiness of pumpkin blends seamlessly with cinnamon, nutmeg, chai, and many other spices so it should be no surprise that the autumn-famous vegetable handles the complexity of curry spice superbly.

First things first: fresh pumpkin is awesome. Don't be intimidated by the notion of cutting up this monster. It's not a jack-o-lantern! Use a long, serrated bread knife and first cut the pumpkin in half lengthwise in a sawing motion. Be safe; don't try to muscle it. Let the teeth of the knife do the work. You can do this pretty easily with a steak knife if necessary. Scoop out the seeds from both sides and place them in a colander. Don't scrape the insides yet! That will make seed cleaning hard and tedious. Rinse the seeds and set them aside—you can tackle the whole seed-toasting thing later (page 125).

Use a melon-baller, a big spoon, or pumpkin scraper and scrape the stringy "guts" out until you hit hard flesh. Do this for both halves then wrap one side in plastic and refrigerate it. The cleaned pumpkin half is good for at least 1 week.

When it comes to peeling you have two choices: Cut the pumpkin in ½-inch cubes then cut the skin off of each cube or peel the pumpkin with a vegetable peeler and then cut it into cubes. If you choose to peel first be sure to peel the pumpkin until the outer flesh is almost as tender as the underside. Just peeling it once like a cucumber will not suffice.

No pumpkin handy? No problem: other squashes like butternut and kabocha are lovely in this recipe as well.

---

8 Cups Better than Bouillon "No Chicken" Chicken Broth or Rich Yellow Vegetable Stock (page 117)

5 cups raw pumpkin, about half of a 5-pound pumpkin, seeded, peeled, and stringy flesh removed, cut into ½-inch cubes

2 tablespoons extra-virgin olive oil

2 small white onions, diced small

2 tablespoons Curry Powder (page 57) or store bought

4 garlic cloves, minced

One 1-inch piece ginger, peeled and minced

3 ounces (about ½ cup) hazelnuts, chopped and toasted in a pan (see method on page 125)

Kosher salt and freshly ground black pepper to taste

Basil Oil (page 56)

(CONTINUED) >

> (CONTINUED FROM PREVIOUS PAGE)

1 In a large stockpot over high heat bring the broth and the pumpkin cubes to a gentle simmer and cook until the pumpkin is very tender (about 20 minutes).

2 While the pumpkin is simmering heat a large skillet over high heat and add the olive oil. When the oil starts to shimmer add the onions and stir until they are golden brown, about 10 minutes. Add the curry powder, garlic, and ginger to the pan and mix in with the onions. Remove the pan from the heat and set it aside. Allow the cooked pumpkin to cool slightly.

3 Place half of the cooked pumpkin in a blender pitcher with as much broth as necessary to puree the soup to a smooth, silky consistency. Return the pureed soup to the pot, add the onion mixture, and stir until completely blended.

4 Place the soup over medium heat just long enough to bring it to a gentle simmer. Season with salt and pepper and adjust the thickness with water if necessary. Ladle the soup into bowls and top with a pinch of toasted hazelnuts and a drizzle of basil oil.

THE SOUP IS GOOD FOR 5 DAYS IN THE FRIDGE AND 2 MONTHS FROZEN.

TIP

When blending hot liquids always use the lid but remove the little fill cap and cover the hole with a folded kitchen towel. The idea is to allow air to escape from the pitcher and prevent the hot liquid from jumping out of the pitcher and causing harm. ("The more you know . . .")

HEARTY MINESTRONE

MAKES 8 SERVINGS

Minestrone is one of those soups that people take for granted—you know, it's often served as a starter in restaurants. But true minestrone is complex; with a heavy ingredient-to-broth ratio, it's really more of a meal especially when you have it with a salad and some crusty bread. Enjoy a big bowl of this soup for dinner—it won't leave you hungry. For something really special: dollop each bowl with a heaping spoonful of Pecan Pesto (page 34).

With all these yummy vegetables I see no need to add pasta to the soup. If you really want some gluten in this dish I recommend toasting a large hand-torn piece of bread and pouring the hot soup over the top. Wow!

2 tablespoons extra-virgin olive oil

1 large white onion, diced small

1 teaspoon dried oregano

1 teaspoon crushed fennel seeds

1 fresh rosemary sprig, stripped and leaves minced

2 celery stalks, cut in half lengthwise then cut thin crosswise

6-ounces smoky tempeh bacon, chopped small (optional)

2 fat carrots, peeled, chopped small

4 garlic cloves, minced

6 firm Roma tomatoes, use the easy-peel method (page 40) then dice, or one 14-ounce can small-diced tomatoes, drained

8 Cups Better than Bouillon "No Beef" Beef Broth or Rich Dark Vegetable Stock (page 117)

One 15-ounce can Great Northern or cannellini beans, drained, or ½ cup dried white beans, soaked and cooked using method 1 or 2 (page 84).

2 zucchini, quartered lengthwise and cut crosswise in ¼-inch slices

1 bunch lacinato kale, inner stems removed, leaves cut in thin, short strips

¼ head savoy or green cabbage, cut in thin, short strips

½ bunch fresh Italian parsley, chopped

10 large fresh basil leaves, chopped

1 Heat a 4-quart saucepan or small stockpot over medium-high heat. Add the olive oil and wait until it shimmers then add the onions and stir with a wooden spoon until they are slightly brown, about 8 minutes.

2 While the onions are browning add the oregano; rub the oregano in your palms to crush the leaves and activate the oils, toss the oregano into the onions and continue cooking. Add the fennel seeds, rosemary, celery, tempeh bacon (if using), carrots, and garlic and stir about 3 minutes more. Stir in the tomatoes and cooked beans then add the broth and bring the soup to a simmer. Add the zucchini, kale, and cabbage and simmer gently for about 10 minutes. Stir in the basil and parsley and serve.

THE SOUP IS GOOD FOR 5 DAYS IN THE FRIDGE AND 2 MONTHS FROZEN.

PASTA FAGIOLI SOUP

This soup is easy to make, kids like it, and a big bowl of it is a meal. It's a perfect fall/winter soup. Traditionally the soup has chopped sausage but let me assure you; it won't be missed. I make up for that sausage flavor with farro grains and ground fennel. The farro delivers a meaty texture and it is high in protein while ground fennel provides that distinct "Italian soup" flavor that makes you feel like you're eating something really hearty. It is important to keep the pasta and soup separate until the last minute. This delivers perfectly cooked pasta and farro and prevents the two from absorbing too much of the liquid.

½ cup farro

2 tablespoons extra-virgin olive oil

1 large white onion, diced medium

2 fat leeks, white parts only, halved lengthwise then rinsed well and sliced thin

1 tablespoon capers, minced

2 teaspoons ground fennel

1 tablespoon dried oregano

3 sprigs fresh thyme, leaves only, chopped, or 1 teaspoon dried

1 sprig fresh rosemary, leaves only, chopped (about a 5-inch sprig)

4 large celery stalks, diced medium

3 medium carrots, peeled, chopped small

4 garlic cloves, minced

8 cups (2 quarts) Better than Bouillon "No Chicken" Chicken Broth or Rich Yellow Vegetable Stock (page 116)

Two 14.5-ounce can kidney beans, drained, or 1 cup dried kidney beans soaked and cooked until tender using method 1 or 2 (page 84)

Kosher salt and freshly ground black pepper to taste

---

1 cup small dried elbow pasta, cooked until tender, drained and reserved

(CONTINUED) >

1 In a small saucepan gently simmer the farro covered in 2 cups of salted water until tender (about 25 minutes). When the farro is cooked drain any excess liquid and reserve the grain off to the side.

2 Heat a large stockpot over medium-high heat. Add the olive oil and wait until it shimmers then add the onions and leeks and stir with a wooden spoon until they are slightly brown, about 8 minutes. When the onions are brown add the capers, fennel, oregano, thyme, rosemary, celery, carrots, and garlic and stir about 3 minutes more. Stir in the broth and bring the soup to a simmer. Add the beans and simmer gently for about 15 minutes.

3 Carefully puree about 2 cups of the soup in a blender until smooth then return the mixture to the soup and adjust the heat to maintain a gentle simmer. Season with salt and pepper to taste. Place two big spoonfuls each of pasta and farro in a large bowl and ladle a healthy portion of hot soup over the top. Give the soup a gentle stir and serve.

THE SOUP IS GOOD FOR 5 DAYS IN THE FRIDGE AND 2 MONTHS FROZEN. DO NOT FREEZE THE SOUP WITH THE PASTA OR FARRO; IT'S BETTER TO REMAKE THEM WHEN YOU DEFROST THE SOUP.

TIP

When blending hot liquids always use the lid but remove the little fill cap and cover the hole with a folded kitchen towel. The idea is to allow air to escape from the pitcher and prevent the hot liquid from jumping out of the pitcher and causing harm. ("The more you know . . .")

ALBONDIGAS SOUP *(Mexican Meatball Soup)*

MAKES 6 SERVINGS

Versions of albondigas soup can be traced all the way back to the sixth century during the Islamic occupation of Spain. Originally, these small meatballs were made of lamb and spices like mint and clove. Some of those flavor profiles disappeared and others remain but the bottom line is that albondigas is a comfort food that is here to stay and to me, nothing beats a big bowl of this soup on a cold day.

TOASTED SPICES:

½ teaspoon ground clove

½ teaspoon cinnamon

1 tablespoon ground cumin

2 teaspoons oregano

ALBONDIGAS:

2 cups dried lentils, about 13 ounces

3 cups Better than Bouillon "No Chicken" Chicken Broth or Rich Yellow Vegetable Stock (page 116)

½ of the toasted spices

1 batch Roberto's Tofu-Rizo (page 10), or one 12-ounce package of Soyrizo (optional)

1 medium white onion, chopped rough

8 ounces button mushrooms

½ cup pecans, blanched almonds, or walnuts

1 tablespoon extra-virgin olive oil

½ cup flaxseed meal

¼ cup all-purpose flour

Kosher salt and freshly ground black pepper to taste

BROTH:

4 large Roma tomatoes, halved, or one 14-ounce can crushed tomatoes

1 tablespoon extra-virgin olive oil

2 medium white or yellow onions, chopped small

4 celery stalks, diced small

4 garlic cloves, minced

Remaining ½ of the toasted spices

8 cups Better than Bouillon "No Chicken" Chicken Broth or Rich Yellow Vegetable Stock (page 116)

1 bunch cilantro, stems included, chopped

Kosher salt and freshly ground black pepper to taste

(CONTINUED) >

NOTE:

This one is a bit more labor intensive but don't let that scare you, it's easy and totally worth it! The broth and the meatballs can be made up 2 days in advance but they must be held separately, as the meatballs tend to get mushy if left in the broth too long.

TOAST THE SPICES

1 Heat a skillet over medium heat. Add all the spices to the dry pan and shake the pan "Jiffy Pop" style until the spices become fragrant and some change color. (This only takes 1 to 2 minutes max.) Continue shaking the pan for about 1 minute after it has been removed from the heat. This will cool the spices and prevent them from burning from residual heat. Set aside.

PREPARE THE ALBONDIGAS

1 Rinse the lentils in cold running water until water runs clear. Pick out any debris. Using a medium soup pot, bring the lentils and broth to a simmer. Cover and cook the lentils until they are very tender and have absorbed most or all of the liquid, about 15 to 20 minutes.

2 Uncover the pot and allow the cooked lentils to cool. Drain any excess liquid. Add half of the toasted spices to the lentil mixture. Add the Tofu-Rizo (if using) to the lentil mixture and stir until well combined. Set aside.

3 Pulse the chopped onion in a food processor until it is finely chopped. Place the onion in a medium bowl and set aside. (Don't clean the food processor yet.) Pulse the mushrooms and nuts in the food processor until they are finely chopped/minced.

4 Heat a medium sauté pan over medium heat and add the tablespoon of olive oil. When the oil is hot add the onion and cook until golden brown then add the mushroom mixture to the pan and sauté an additional 5 minutes.

5 Place the cooked lentils and the onion mixture in a large bowl and mash them with a potato masher or a fork. Using a wooden spoon or a rubber spatula stir in the flaxseed meal and flour until the mixture comes together and resembles a crumbly dough. Taste and season well with salt and pepper. Refrigerate the lentil mixture for about 30 minutes to firm up. (While the albondigas mixture is in the fridge, make the soup broth.)

6 After the mixture has firmed up, shape it into little balls (a little smaller than a golf ball). Place the albondigas in a sauté pan with a few dashes of olive oil. Over medium heat, brown the meatballs on all sides (about 30 seconds per side). Do this in batches if necessary. Place the albondigas on a plate or small sheet tray and cover them with foil to keep them warm until assembly.

PREPARE THE BROTH

1 Preheat the broiler and line a sheet tray with foil. Place the halved tomatoes cut side down on the sheet tray and place them in the broiler until the skins blister or char, about 5 minutes. Using a pair of tongs remove the charred skins from the tomatoes and discard them. Let tomatoes cool. Roughly chop the tomatoes, being careful to reserve all the pulp and juice. Place the liquid and chopped tomatoes in a small bowl.

2 Heat a medium soup pot over high heat. Add the olive oil and wait until it shimmers then add the chopped onions and stir with a wooden spoon until they are slightly brown (about 8 minutes). Add the celery, garlic, and tomatoes and stir for about 3 minutes more. Pour in the broth and remaining toasted spices then bring the soup to a gentle simmer. Allow the broth to simmer for 10 to 15 minutes. Stir in the chopped cilantro and season the broth with salt and pepper.

ASSEMBLE

1 Place about four warm albondigas in each soup bowl and pour a generous amount of broth over the top. Serve immediately.

MEATBALLS AND BROTH ARE GOOD FOR 5 DAYS REFRIGERATED OR 2 MONTHS FROZEN. YOU CAN FREEZE THE BROTH AND MEATBALLS SEPARATELY. DEFROST THE MEATBALLS SLOWLY BY PLACING THEM IN THE REFRIGERATOR OVERNIGHT.

RED BERRY SOUP

MAKES 8 SERVINGS

This is the BEST thing to serve as a first course on a warm evening because it is sweet, cold, and very refreshing and it accompanies any crisp white wine or bubbly perfectly. You can also serve this as a light dessert after a spicy and hearty meal like the Baingan Bhartha (page 201). The tiny invisible tapioca balls make the soup unique and almost look like red champagne.

3 pints ripe strawberries, washed and stems removed

1 pint raspberries, washed

Juice of ½ lemon

3 cups water

¾ cup organic white sugar

¾ cup granulated tapioca (not pearl)

1 teaspoon vanilla extract

1 cup sweet white wine

Fresh mint for serving

1 Place the strawberries, raspberries, and lemon juice in a blender or food processor with 1 cup of water. Puree. If you want a completely smooth soup, strain the puree to remove the strawberry seeds. Place the puree in a bowl, cover, and chill.

2 Place 2 cups of water in a medium saucepan. Add the sugar and stir. Bring the sugar water to a gentle simmer over medium heat and add the tapioca. Cook the tapioca over medium-low heat for about 10 minutes or until almost all the granules are invisible. Stir in the vanilla extract and wine and remove the pan from the heat.

3 In a large bowl or plastic pitcher combine the tapioca and berry puree and whisk to break apart all the little gummy clumps. Chill thoroughly—you'll want to serve this cold.

4 Ladle portions of about 5 ounces into shallow bowls and garnish with fresh mint.

SOUP IS GOOD FOR A WEEK REFRIGERATED BUT THICKENS OVER TIME; YOU CAN ADD WATER OR ORANGE JUICE TO THIN IT OUT. I DON'T RECOMMEND FREEZING THIS SOUP: THE TAPIOCA GETS WEIRD (GUMMY) WHEN DEFROSTED.

NOTE:

You can hold the wine from the soup and serve it to kids, then add the wine to the rest of the soup for the grown-ups . . . I've done that many times.

HOT STOCK TIPS: PREPARING, STRAINING, AND COOLING

A rich, flavorful stock is the foundation of any good soup, sauce, or stew. While its preparation is not to be taken lightly, it is really easy to make. In the non-vegan world stocks can take days, but with veggies it only takes about an hour to an hour and a half of simmering before all the flavor has been extracted from the vegetables. Simmering longer will not improve the final product, in fact, it could ruin it. If the vegetables are simmered to a mush you will end up with a watery carrot soup that is not strainable, which is exactly what most store-bought vegetable stocks taste like to me.

Here are a few stock tips:

QUANTITY: THE CHEF'S RULE OF THUMB

Regardless of the quantity of stock you are making the "chef's rule of thumb" is 50 percent of celery plus 50 percent of carrots should equal 100% of onion. For example: if using 1 pound of onion you should use ½ pound of celery and ½ pound of carrot. Or 2 cups onion, 1 cup celery, and 1 cup carrot. The rest is pretty hard to screw up. Be sure to add some garlic in whatever form you have; fresh is always better but in a pinch granulated or powder is OK, too. You should throw in some parsley and whatever herbs you can get your hands on . . . cilantro, basil, a little bit of rosemary, a sage leaf . . . it's all good. To calculate how much water to use simply double the amount of stock you want to end up with.

SAVE YOUR SCRAPS

When preparing a meal there are always left-over veggie pieces that normally end up in the trash. With very little effort these scraps can be turned into stock.

- When peeling an onion discard the paperlike skin but those next two layers should be saved for stock.

- When peeling carrots, peel the whole carrot from tip to end then cut off 1 inch on both ends and save those ends.

- Remove the celery hearts, ends, and bulbs then wash and save them.

- Root vegetables like celeriac, parsnips, and ruta-bagas should get peeled with a veg peeler then cut into huge cubes before cutting as directed. All these trimmings are awesome for stock.

- Leftover grilled vegetables (especially mushrooms) are terrific.

If you have enough of these scraps saved up in one week add them to your stock along with the recipe ingredients. Not making stock right away? Freeze your scraps as they come along and when you finally get around to making a stock dig them up and plop them in once the stock is at a simmer.

STRAINING

I'm very sensitive to the fact that not everyone has a huge strainer in their kitchen and even fewer own a chinois. I've also been told that some folks are under the impression that a colander and a strainer are, if not the same thing, at least interchangeable. They are neither. A strainer of any size is made of some form of mesh whereas a colander is a bowl with holes. (If you use a colander, you're going to be courting a huge mess. And perhaps a burn—no joke). If you don't have a big strainer a good technique is to use a skimmer or slotted spoon to remove vegetables then strain the stock through a small strainer or 1 sheet of cheesecloth.

COOLING HOT STOCK

Improperly cooling hot liquids can be ground zero for foodborne illness. It's not that dangerous for home cooks because the quantities people make at home are usually small. However, you'll want to follow proper steps (safe, sorry, etc.). Never place a hot stock directly into the fridge. The hot stock will raise the overall temperature of the fridge and everything in the fridge along with it. The stock will take a long time to cool down to a safe temperature and in the meantime bacteria can run amuck.

One good way of avoiding a bacteria frenzy is to follow these steps:

1 Allow the stock to cool to room temperature outside the fridge.

2 Place it uncovered in the fridge until cold.

3 When the stock is nice and cold, cover it.

The downside to this is it takes a while and a good deal of attention. My favorite technique is to strain the stock then return it to the pot and simmer it about 20 minutes longer to reduce the volume by a few cups then quickly cool the stock with plenty of ice. When the stock is cool to the touch it is safe to be refrigerated.

STOCK IS GENERALLY GOOD FOR 1 WEEK REFRIGERATED OR 3 MONTHS FROZEN.

RICH YELLOW VEGETABLE STOCK

MAKES 6 CUPS

This is my version of a no-chicken chicken broth. Although this is not a dark stock, I like to brown the onions slightly to extract some of their flavor and sugars. Leeks are great because their flavor is earthy and subtle, but if you don't have them or don't want to use them, it's not the end of the world.

2 tablespoons high-heat oil, like grapeseed or safflower

2 large white or brown onions, peeled, halved, and cut into ¼-inch-thick slices

2 leeks, light green and white parts only, cut in 2-inch pieces and rinsed clean (optional)

12 cups cool water

2 Roma tomatoes, halved

4 celery ribs, cut into ½-inch pieces

3 medium carrots, peeled and cut into ½-inch pieces

4 large garlic cloves, crushed

3 fresh thyme sprigs or 1 teaspoon dried thyme

1 handful fresh flat-leaf parsley leaves and stems

1 cup sliced button mushrooms

1 teaspoon ground turmeric

Vegetable trimmings (if available)

1 tablespoon kosher salt

½ teaspoon freshly ground black pepper

1 Heat the oil in a 5-quart or larger stockpot over high heat. Add the onions and leeks (if using) and stir with a wooden spoon for 8 to 10 minutes or until they show signs of color. Stir in the water and all the remaining ingredients and bring the liquid to a boil. Adjust the heat to maintain a gentle simmer. Simmer the stock uncovered for 1 hour.

2 Remove the pot from the heat and carefully strain the stock into an 8-cup measuring pitcher or large bowl (see straining and cooling hot stock, page 114). Press gently on the solids in the strainer to extract the entire flavor. If necessary, return the stock to the same stockpot and simmer until reduced to 6 cups.

3 Allow the stock to cool to room temperature uncovered then refrigerate it uncovered until cold. When the refrigerated stock is cold, transfer it to a mason jar or similar container with a fitted lid.

STOCK IS GOOD FOR 1 WEEK REFRIGERATED OR 3 MONTHS FROZEN.

RICH DARK VEGETABLE STOCK

MAKES 6 CUPS

This is my version of a no-beef beef broth. The key to a rich dark vegetable stock is in browning the onions. Browning occurs when any ingredient is heated enough to release its sugars. These sugars burn and create a dark caramel seasoning (the stock's source of sugar and color). Along with the wine, other vegetables, and aromatics, the caramelized onions provide the stock with deep, rich flavor that is distinctly different from a stock made of the same ingredients that has been simply boiled.

---

2 tablespoons high-heat oil, like grapeseed or safflower

2 large white or brown onions, peeled, halved, and cut into ¼-inch-thick slices

1 cup sliced button mushrooms, plus any dark mushroom trimmings or soaking liquid

2 cups cheap red wine

12 cups cool water

2 tablespoons vegan Worcestershire sauce

4 Roma tomatoes, halved

4 celery ribs, cut into ½-inch pieces

3 medium carrots, peeled and cut into ½-inch pieces

4 large garlic cloves, crushed

5 fresh thyme sprigs or 1 teaspoon dried thyme

1 handful fresh flat-leaf parsley leaves and stems

Vegetable trimmings (if available)

1 tablespoon kosher salt

½ teaspoon freshly ground black pepper

1   Heat the oil in a 5-quart or larger stockpot over high heat. Add the onions and sauté them for 15 to 20 minutes, stirring often with a wooden spoon to prevent scorching. The onions should be a deep brown color with specks of black char.

2   Carefully add the red wine and deglaze the bottom of the pot by scraping any bits of onion that might be stuck.

3   Allow the wine to simmer until it is almost gone. Stir in the water and all the remaining ingredients and bring the liquid to a boil. Adjust the heat to maintain a gentle simmer. Simmer the stock uncovered for 1 hour.

4   Remove the pot from the heat and carefully strain the stock into an 8-cup measuring pitcher or large bowl (see straining and cooling hot stock, page 114). Press gently on the solids in the strainer to extract the entire flavor. If necessary, return the stock to the same pot and simmer until reduced to 6 cups.

5   Allow the stock to cool to room temperature uncovered then refrigerate it uncovered until cold. When the refrigerated stock is cold, transfer it to a mason jar or similar container with a fitted lid.

STOCK IS GOOD FOR 1 WEEK REFRIGERATED OR 3 MONTHS FROZEN.

5 | TREAT YOUR GREENS RIGHT

BEST KALE SALAD EVER

MAKES 6 SERVINGS

Kale salads are everywhere these days and most of them are used as vehicles for dressing. Tahini-drenched kale? I say kale-no! Here the kale flavor is featured by serving it raw and pairing it with grilled cabbage to deliver a smoky-crunch winning salad that has orange sweetness without a ton of dressing. The pepitas offer a salty crunch with earthy undertones and the sweetness of the cranberries balances out bitterness that the raw kale imparts.

2 large bunches lacinato kale

½ head Napa cabbage

4 long, fat carrots, peeled then cut into ribbons with a vegetable peeler

1 yellow bell pepper, cut into thin strips

½ bunch scallions, green parts only, sliced thin

½ cup dried cranberries

Juice of 1 orange

3 tablespoons apple cider vinegar

3 tablespoons extra-virgin olive oil

Kosher salt and freshly ground black pepper

½ cup pepitas (toasted and salted pumpkin seeds) plus extra for garnish (page 125)

1 Wash and pat the kale dry. Using a sharp paring knife, remove and discard the tough ribs that run in between each leaf of kale. Stack the leaves and cut them crosswise into strips.

2 Cut off the bottom of the cabbage and separate each leaf. Wash and pat the leaves dry. Turn on an exhaust fan if you have one and heat a grill pan or cast-iron skillet over high heat. (You want the pan blazing hot.) Working in batches, grill/char the cabbage leaves. Use a spatula to press the cabbage leaves down against the hot pan. Place the grilled cabbage onto a sheet tray or large plate to cool. When the cabbage leaves are cool enough to handle, stack and cut them crosswise into thin strips.

3 In a large bowl add all of the ingredients and season with salt and pepper then toss the salad thoroughly. Cover and let the salad rest 20 to 30 minutes in the refrigerator to soften the kale and allow the flavors to meld. After the salad has rested place it in a colander to remove excess liquid and dressing. Garnish the salad with additional pepitas and serve immediately.

THE SALAD IS AT ITS BEST WHEN EATEN THE DAY IT WAS MADE BUT STILL YUMMY FOR ABOUT 3 DAYS AFTER.

GRILLED NAPA SALAD

This is a take on a classic Italian calamari salad. The flavor combinations and colors are outstanding and unlike most salads, this one is even better the next few days. If you can't find oyster mushrooms use something else like portabella or even button mushrooms if necessary.

This is the salad that will win over your foodie friends who think vegan food is boring. It proves that nothing is lost by going vegan. Good food is all around. I would eat this salad every day if I could.

Extra-virgin olive oil as needed

1 large Napa cabbage

Kosher salt and freshly ground black pepper to taste

2 medium fennel bulbs

1 yellow bell pepper, seeded and cut into ¼-inch strips

8 ounces oyster mushrooms, cut in half along the stem

½ medium red onion, sliced very thin, rinsed in cold water then patted dry

1½ cups pitted Kalamata olives, quartered lengthwise

2 cups organic cherry or grape tomatoes, halved or quartered if large

2 celery ribs, sliced thin

---

1 batch Mediterranean Dressing (page 52)

1 Remove the bottom of the cabbage and separate the leaves. Rinse the leaves and pat them dry. In a large bowl toss the leaves in olive oil, salt, and pepper then set them aside.

2 Prep the fennel by trimming off the protruding stems from the bulb, leaving one inch or so on the bulb. Cut the fennel bulbs in half lengthwise and slice them into ¼-inch strips crosswise. Place the fennel slices in a large bowl with the bell pepper and mushrooms then toss them with olive oil, salt, and pepper.

3 Turn on an exhaust fan if you have one and heat a grill pan or cast-iron pan over high heat. (You want the pan blazing hot.) Working in batches, grill/char the cabbage leaves. Use a spatula to press the cabbage leaves down against the hot pan. Place the grilled cabbage onto a sheet tray or large plate to cool. Grill/char the fennel mixture in the same fashion as above and place them in a large bowl to cool.

4 When the cabbage is cool enough to handle cut it crosswise into ¼-inch strips and add it to the grilled fennel mixture. Toss the grilled vegetable mixture with the red onion, olives, tomatoes, and celery. Pour all the dressing over the salad and toss to coat. Season the salad with salt and pepper. Allow the salad to chill and marinate in the fridge for 30 minutes to overnight.

THE SALAD IS GOOD FOR 4-5 DAYS REFRIGERATED.

CHOPPED BEET SALAD *with* BEET TOPS

MAKES 6 SERVINGS

Use any variety of beets you like for this salad; the magic happens in the cooling and marinating process. As the beets cool they shrivel a bit and this traps the dressing in their outer layer, giving the beet a salty, complex flavor. The peppery tone of the arugula and crisp tartness of the apple balance the sweet and earthy flavor of the beets perfectly. Crazy-good salad.

1 batch Beet Salad Vinaigrette (page 50)

6 large beets, stems and leaves attached

1 tablespoon extra-virgin olive oil

2 Fuji apples, cored and diced medium

3 cups baby arugula

Kosher salt and freshly ground black pepper to taste

1 cup toasted pecan pieces (see method on page 125)

1 Make the vinaigrette first.

2 Preheat the oven to 400°F. Line a baking tray with parchment paper.

3 Wash the beets and beet tops well. Slice the beet tops very thin and set them aside. Discard the stems or save them for juicing. Peel the beets with a vegetable peeler then dice them into ¼-inch cubes and toss them with the olive oil. Roast the beets in a single layer on the baking tray for 10 minutes or until they are tender.

4 While the beets are hot place them in a medium bowl and toss them with just enough vinaigrette to coat. Place the beets in the fridge to marinate and chill 30 minutes to 1 day.

ASSEMBLY

1 In a large bowl gently combine the beets, beet tops, apples, and arugula. Season the salad with salt and pepper.

2 Mound about 1 cup of salad onto a medium plate. Top the salad with toasted pecans and a drizzle of additional vinaigrette.

SALAD IS GOOD FOR 3 TO 4 DAYS BUT THE GREENS WILL BE EXTREMELY SOGGY.

PROPERLY TOASTING NUTS AND SPICES

The most common thing burned in a professional kitchen is nuts (heh-heh). But seriously . . . the reasons are pretty basic: we're trying to do something else while toasting the nuts or spices, the heat is too high, or we don't keep agitating the pan even after it has been removed from the heat.

Of course nuts can be toasted in an oven but I'm not a big fan. It's inconsistent. Not all sides of the nuts are exposed equally to heat and without agitation you end up with inconsistencies. Here's the best way:

Heat a dry skillet over medium heat. Add the spices or nuts to the dry pan and shake the pan "Jiffy Pop" style until the spices or nuts become fragrant and start to change color. (This only takes 1 to 2 minutes maximum for spices but it can take 4 to 6 minutes for nuts, depending on their size.)

Continue shaking the pan for 1 to 2 minutes after it has been removed from the heat. This will cool the spices or nuts and prevent them from burning from residual heat.

IN GENERAL, TOASTED NUTS WILL LAST 1 MONTH STORED IN AN AIRTIGHT CONTAINER. SPICES WILL LAST 6 MONTHS STORED IN AN AIRTIGHT CONTAINER.

BEET CARPACCIO *with* ARUGULA *and* MISO DRESSING

MAKES 8 SERVINGS

I'm just going to say it: OMG do I love beets. They are crazy good for you and one of the most colorful vegetables you can serve. They're also pretty versatile; this is just one of many ways to serve beets in a salad. Use this preparation as a guide and enjoy all colors and sizes with any dressing you like.

5 medium beets (any color)

1 tablespoon extra-virgin olive oil

4 cups organic baby arugula

Kosher salt and freshly ground black pepper to taste

1 batch Miso Dressing (page 53)

1 Preheat oven to 425°F.

2 Trim, wash, and dry the beet tops. Save the tops for another salad or wilt them as you would spinach. Cut and discard the root ends and wash the beets well. Rub the beets with the olive oil and place them on a foil-lined sheet tray. Cover the beets loosely with foil and bake them for 30 to 45 minutes or until they can be pierced easily with a skewer. Uncover and remove the beets from the oven. Allow the beets to cool completely while you make the dressing.

3 When the beets are cool, rub the skins off with a paper towel. Using a knife or mandolin, slice the beets crosswise as thin as possible. This salad can be made in advance up to this point and held in the fridge until needed.

ASSEMBLY

1 In a medium bowl, toss the arugula with about 4 tablespoons of Miso Dressing.

2 Arrange the beet slices equally on large salad plates. Distribute an equal amount of arugula on each plate in the center of the beets and season the greens with salt and pepper. Drizzle a bit of dressing over beets as well and serve immediately. This salad can easily be served family style on a large platter as well.

NOTE:

Unless you want to look like Dexter, you'll want to wear rubber gloves when preparing beets because they can stain your hands. They also tend to stain wooden cutting boards but chill, it's not permanent: the stain disappears after a few washings.

HERBACEOUS *and* NUTTY WHEAT BERRY SALAD

MAKES 6 SERVINGS

Wheat berries are whole unprocessed wheat kernels. They are super good for you because they contain the germ, endosperm, and bran (which means they are a terrific source of protein and fiber). Now that I've got my eighth-grade agriculture report out of the way, here's why wheat berries are great: they have a dense, meaty texture that is easy to complement and are filling. Did I mention they taste great? The mint and nuts are what make this salad sing. Not too many salads hold up the next few days but because the wheat berry is so hearty, it stands up nicely for a while—just keep the lettuce separate.

2 cups wheat berries

3 celery ribs, diced small

¼ cup pistachios, toasted and chopped

¼ cup pecan pieces, toasted and chopped

½ cup dried currants

10 large mint leaves, sliced in thin strips

½ bunch scallions, green parts only, cut very thin

Killer Blood Orange Vinaigrette (page 51)

2 small heads butter lettuce, cut into 1-inch pieces, washed and spun dry, held cold with a wet paper towel over the top

Kosher salt and freshly ground black pepper to taste

1 In a large saucepan over high heat combine the wheat berries and enough water to come 3 inches over the wheat berries. Bring the liquid to a boil and reduce the heat to a simmer. Cook the wheat berries covered for 45 minutes to 1 hour until the grain is tender but resistant to the bite. Drain any excess liquid and allow the wheat berries to cool.

2 When the wheat berries are cool toss them in a large bowl with the celery, nuts, currants, and herbs. Dress the salad with a healthy amount of vinaigrette and let it sit at least 15 minutes to allow the flavors to amalgamate.

3 Just before serving add the lettuce and toss. Season with salt and pepper. Store any unused lettuce separately from the wheat berry salad.

THE SALAD IS GOOD FOR 4 DAYS IN THE REFRIGERATOR.

CELERIAC SALAD

MAKES 6 SERVINGS

Raw celeriac has a subtle earthy flavor that is super refreshing. This salad could not be any easier to make. If you've never worked with celeriac, it's pretty straightforward. The first thing you need to do is peel this creature. I recommend cutting the outside away with a knife exposing the white flesh, then clean it up with a vegetable peeler. Give the celeriac a rinse and clean the cutting board before cutting the celeriac into match sticks or grating it with a box grater. Serve this any time coleslaw would be appropriate, like with my Bad Boy Pulled Barbecue Sandwiches (page 85).

¼ cup Basic Mayo (page 36), or store-bought vegan mayonnaise

¼ cup Dijon mustard

Zest and juice of 1 lemon

½ bunch flat-leaf parsley, chopped

2 pounds celery root, peeled and cut into small matchsticks or grated

2 large green apples, peeled, cored, and cut into small matchsticks or grated

Kosher salt and freshly ground black pepper to taste

1 Combine the mayonnaise, mustard, lemon zest, lemon juice, and parsley in a large bowl.

2 Fold in the celery root and apple until the salad is well combined. Season with salt and pepper.

3 Cover the salad and refrigerate until chilled, at least 1 hour before serving.

SALAD IS GOOD FOR 5 DAYS.

CURRIED CHICKPEA SALAD

MAKES 6 SERVINGS

This protein-packed, uber-simple recipe is ideal for taking to work for a lunch on a bed of greens, in a butter lettuce cup, or just eaten with crackers. It can be used as a sandwich filler, a wrap, or scooped onto seasoned sliced tomatoes when they are in season. It's super versatile. My nine-year-old likes it, and that's saying something.

1 cup dried chickpeas, soaked using method 1 or 2 (page 84) then cooked until very tender, or two 15-ounce cans chickpeas, drained and rinsed

3 celery ribs, diced small

1 large organic Granny Smith apple, peeled and diced small

½ cup toasted chopped pecans

½ cup currants or raisins

⅓ cup Basic Mayo (page 36), or store-bought vegan mayonnaise

1 tablespoon Curry Powder (page 57) or store bought

2 tablespoons agave syrup

2 whole scallions, green parts thinly sliced and white parts minced

1 large garlic clove, minced

Kosher salt and freshly ground black pepper to taste

1 Place half of the chickpeas in a food processor and pulse them once or twice to chop them up a bit. (This can also be done in a bowl with a potato masher.)

2 Place the chickpeas and the rest of the salad ingredients in a large bowl and mix them with a rubber spatula until well combined.

3 Season the salad with salt and pepper then cover and refrigerate it for 30 minutes minimum before serving.

SALAD IS GOOD FOR 5 DAYS IN THE REFRIGERATOR.

GOBO ROOT, HARICOTS VERTS, *and* HAZELNUT SALAD

MAKES 4 SERVINGS

If you are not familiar with gobo root (also called burdock root), let me be the first to tell you how awesome it is. Gobo is really good for you; it's been said it helps regulate blood-sugar levels, lower cholesterol, and help with psoriasis, eczema, and overall longevity. That's pretty cool for an ugly root; it really looks just like a small tree root you might find growing in your backyard. It has an earthy dirt flavor when eaten raw but when cooked, it blossoms with a rich, nutty, and buttery flavor.

You should be available to find gobo at your local grocery store but if not, check out Asian markets and health food stores. It peels easily like a carrot and it browns immediately, which is why I recommend placing it in water (don't worry if it browns on you; it will not affect the flavor in any way).

2 gobo (about four 8-inch pieces)

2 fat carrots, peeled

1 tablespoons extra-virgin olive oil

½ cup water

2 tablespoons rice wine vinegar

½ pound haricots verts (French green beans), ends trimmed

2 organic oranges

Kosher salt and freshly ground black pepper to taste

3 ounces (about ½ cup) hazelnuts, chopped and toasted in a pan (see method on page 125)

Basic Vinaigrette (page 49)

1 Fill a medium bowl with cool water and set it aside.

2 Peel the gobo root then wash it thoroughly. Cut the root into 4-inch pieces then cut the pieces into matchsticks. Hold the cut gobo root in the bowl of water until ready to cook. Cut the carrot just like the gobo root and set it aside separately from the root. (Only cut as much carrot as needed to equal the amount of gobo root.)

3 Heat a large skillet over medium-high heat, add the olive oil, and wait for it to shimmer. Drain water from the gobo root and carefully add it to the pan and toss it for a few minutes then add the ½ cup water and rice vinegar and simmer until the liquid is almost gone, about 5 minutes. Add the carrots and cook a few minutes more.

4 Remove from heat, drain any leftover liquid, and place the gobo root mixture in a bowl to cool then refrigerate until cold. (Note: the carrot will be tender but not completely cooked.)

5 While the gobo and carrot are chilling prep the haricots verts. Bring a large pot of heavily salted water to a rolling boil and prepare a large bowl of ice water. Add the beans to the boiling water and blanch, uncovered, until crisp-tender, about 2 minutes. (The cooking time will vary according to the beans, amount of water, etc.) Remove

(CONTINUED) >

PROPERLY SEGMENTING ORANGES, LEMONS, AND GRAPEFRUIT

You may be thinking, "Why do I need technique? You just peel and cut, right?" Not so fast, my friend. If you want to avoid fruit that looks like you've used your kindergartener's scissors to cut it, use this method. And practice, practice, practice.

Cut the top and bottom off the citrus fruit and trim away the peel and pith with a sharp knife, exposing the flesh of the orange. (Be sure to do this in a rounded fashion, not straight down.)

Holding the fruit in one hand, carefully make an incision against but parallel to the connective membrane down to the center of the fruit.

Make your second cut within the same segment on the other side against the connective membrane, freeing the orange segment and allowing it to fall onto the cutting board.

Continue in this fashion until all the segments are removed.

Save the segments on a paper towel so they aren't too wet when being plated.

SEGMENTS CAN BE STORED FOR UP TO 2 DAYS IN THE FRIDGE.

> (CONTINUED FROM PREVIOUS PAGE)

the beans with a skimmer or drain them in a colander and plunge them into the ice water for about 2 minutes only to stop the cooking process. Do not leave the beans in the ice water too long or they will get soggy. Drain the beans and pat them dry with a kitchen towel or paper towels. Place the green beans in the fridge to chill completely.

6 Peel and segment the oranges then hold them in the fridge until assembly (see method to the left to segment an orange the kewl chef way). Although it's best the same day, the ingredients can be left in the fridge a day or two before assembly.

ASSEMBLY

1 In a large bowl toss the gobo root and carrots with all the vinaigrette. Coat the gobo and carrots thoroughly then remove them with a pair of tongs and place them in a small bowl.

2 Place the green beans in the dressing bowl; toss the beans in the remaining vinaigrette and season aggressively with salt and pepper.

3 Mound one-quarter of the green beans in the center of a large plate and top them with one-quarter of the gobo root mixture. Top the salad with some orange segments and a healthy portion of chopped hazelnuts. Serve immediately.

THE SALAD IS A LITTLE SOGGY THE NEXT DAY BUT STILL QUITE GOOD.

SHAVED FENNEL *with* ARUGULA CRUNCH SALAD

MAKES 4 SERVINGS

This mind-blowing salad has that satisfying crunch that we crave so often, but the gastrique is the real star here: It balances sweet and tart wonderfully to marinate and soften the fennel to perfection. It's easy to make and a great switch from the usual vinaigrette.

Orange Gastrique (page 48)

4 medium fennel bulbs, cleaned and trimmed to bulbs only, fronds chopped and reserved

1 large Granny Smith apple

⅓ cup chives, cut in ¼-inch pieces

Kosher salt and freshly ground black pepper to taste

4 cups baby arugula

½ cup salted and toasted sunflower seeds

1 Make the gastrique first.

2 Cut the fennel bulbs in half lengthwise and shave them really thin with a mandolin, starting with the tops down to the base. (If you don't have a mandolin, do your best with a sharp knife.) Peel, halve, and core the apple then slice it thin crosswise.

3 In a medium bowl toss the shaved fennel, apple slices, and chives with the orange gastrique. Season the mixture with salt and pepper. Cover and let the salad marinate 30 minutes to one day.

ASSEMBLY

1 On a salad plate place about ¼ cup of the fennel salad and top the fennel with a fat pinch of arugula and then sprinkle generously with sunflower seeds then top the arugula with more fennel salad and more seeds. Serve immediately.

STORE ANY UNUSED ARUGULA SEPARATE FROM THE FENNEL SALAD. THE FENNEL SALAD IS GOOD FOR 5 DAYS IN THE REFRIGERATOR.

BLACKENED PLUM TOMATOES
over CUCUMBER *and* FENNEL SALAD

MAKES 6 SERVINGS

If I could put only one salad in this book, this would be it! There is a lot going on here but the end result is harmonious; truly a symphony of simple flavors coming together to make something special. I really like Paul Prudhomme's blackened spices—they're perfect for blackening anything like tofu and eggplant.

In my opinion, fennel is a totally underused veg. What I love about fennel is that in addition to being really good for you, it can be very versatile. It's great in soups and purees but it stands up to grilling, too. Here it's served raw but it is sliced thin and marinated so it softens and adds a lovely balance to the cucumber and mint, which in turn offset the heat of the blackened tomato.

6 really firm Roma tomatoes

4 tablespoons Cajun spice (any one of Paul Prudhomme's blackened spices)

4 tablespoons extra-virgin olive oil or as needed

3 tablespoons sugar

⅓ cup rice wine vinegar

3 hothouse cucumbers, peeled

2 large fennel bulbs, trimmed

¼ cup (2 ounces) pickled ginger, minced

½ bunch scallions, green parts only, sliced very thin on the bias

½ bunch fresh mint leaves, stacked and sliced into thin ribbons

10 large basil leaves, stacked and sliced into thin ribbons

Kosher salt and freshly ground black pepper to taste

Wasabi Aioli (page 35)
Sweet Soy Glaze (page 45)

1 Slice the tomatoes into ⅓-inch slices and discard the end pieces or save them for stock. Firmly press the tomato slices dry between a paper towel–lined kitchen towel. Sprinkle a few tablespoons of blackening spice on a small plate then press one side of each tomato into the spice and set the tomato spice side up onto a plate. Repeat the process until all the tomatoes have been seasoned. (Use more than one plate if necessary.)

2 Heat a large cast-iron pan or skillet over high heat and sprinkle it with kosher salt. When the pan is hot add about 2 tablespoons of olive oil and wait until the oil shimmers. It is important that the oil is hot or the spices will stick to the pan and the tomatoes will be bare and *that's no bueno!* Carefully place the tomatoes spice side down in the pan and blacken one side only for about 2 minutes. Using a fish spatula or a pair of tongs, return the tomatoes to the large plate and allow them to cool. Use the remaining olive oil to blacken the remaining tomatoes. When the tomatoes are no longer hot place them in the refrigerator to chill.

3 In a large bowl whisk the sugar and vinegar until the sugar is dissolved. Using a mandolin or a sharp knife, slice the cucumbers crosswise very thin (about ¹⁄₁₆ inch or thinner). Add the cucumbers to the vinegar

and sugar mixture. Slice the fennel bulbs in the same fashion and add them to the cucumber mixture. Add the pickled ginger, scallions, mint, and basil and combine thoroughly. Season the salad with salt and pepper. Cover the bowl and place it in the refrigerator for at least 30 minutes and up to 2 days. Make the Wasabi Aioli and Sweet Soy Glaze and hold them both chilled.

ASSEMBLY

1 Drain the liquid from the cucumber-fennel salad in a colander. Squeeze the salad firmly in a lint-free towel or a paper towel—lined kitchen towel to remove as much of the liquid as possible. Discard the liquid.

2 Mound about ¾ cup of the cucumber-fennel salad in the center of a medium plate. Bank three blackened tomatoes on the mound of salad. Drizzle the bottom one-third of the blackened tomatoes with the aioli. Drizzle the exposed cucumber fennel salad with the glaze. Repeat the process with the remaining plates and serve at once.

TOMATOES ARE GOOD FOR 3 DAYS AND CUCUMBER-FENNEL SALAD IS GOOD FOR 1 WEEK REFRIGERATED.

EGGPLANT PÂTÉ *on* ENDIVE

MAKES 3 CUPS PÂTÉ

I enjoyed sharing pâté and red wine with friends and I really wanted to come up with something that was rich and satisfying and not made from force-fed animals. If you like the elusive umami flavor as much as I do, you will flip your lid the first time you try this intoxicating concoction. The pâté is great on toasted French bread slices, crackers, or as a sandwich spread with lettuce and tomato . . . in fact, it is so delicious and complex you really could just serve it on teaspoons.

---

1 large eggplant

Extra-virgin olive oil as needed

8 ounces shiitake mushrooms, washed and quartered with stems

2 garlic cloves, minced

2 tablespoons brown sugar

2 tablespoons balsamic vinegar

2 tablespoons soy sauce

4 ounces (½ cup) vegan butter, cut into cubes and softened slightly

Freshly ground black pepper to taste

4 Belgian endive

½ yellow bell pepper, minced

2 tablespoons chopped scallions, green parts only

1 Cut the eggplant crosswise into ¼-inch slices. Brush both sides of each slice with olive oil and set the slices aside.

2 Preheat an outdoor grill, broiler, or grill pan until very hot. Grill or broil the eggplant slices until soft, dark, and charred on both sides then set them on a plate to cool. Note: You want to focus on cooking the eggplant thoroughly while creating good char marks for added flavor. Forget about their appearance and don't worry if they get ripped in half.

3 Heat a large skillet over medium-high heat then add a drizzle of olive oil to the pan and wait for it to shimmer. Add the mushrooms and toss until the mushrooms are wilted, about 5 minutes.

3 Place the eggplant slices, mushrooms, garlic, sugar, vinegar, and soy sauce in the bowl of your food processor fitted with the S blade. Pulse the mixture until smooth, stopping a few times to scrape down the sides. With machine running, feed the softened butter into the pâté a few cubes at a time and continue to run until fully incorporated. Season the pâté with pepper. Place the pâté in a container and refrigerate 30 minutes. Serve dollops on the end of individual endive leaves and garnish with bell pepper and scallions.

PÂTÈ IS GOOD FOR 1 WEEK REFRIGERATED.

6 | A LITTLE SUMTHIN-SUMTHIN ON THE SIDE

LEEK *and* CAULIFLOWER MUFFINS

MAKES 12 MUFFINS

Leek and cauliflower are two tastes that go great together (and you thought that description was just for peanut butter and chocolate). Gratin, soup, and . . . muffins! Mushrooms add extra texture and flavor to these savory muffins; they are a great accompaniment to a simple salad or soup.

4 tablespoons extra-virgin olive oil

1 head of cauliflower

2 fat leeks

8 ounces button mushrooms, sliced thin

3 garlic cloves, minced

3 tablespoons chives, minced

1 cup flaxseed meal

1½ cups Daiya cheddar cheese or similar (optional)

Kosher salt and freshly ground black pepper to taste

1 Preheat the oven to 425°F. Grease twelve large cupcake tins with 2 tablespoons of olive oil.

2 Trim the cauliflower into small equally sized florets. Using a large stockpot, bring 3 quarts of water to rolling boil. Simmer the cauliflower florets until they are tender, about 8 minutes. Drain the water and spread the florets out on a kitchen towel to cool off and dry. Chop the cooked cauliflower into roughly ½-inch pieces and place it in a large bowl.

3 Cut the leeks in half lengthwise then cut them into thin strips crosswise. Rinse the sliced leeks thoroughly to remove any dirt.

4 Heat a large skillet or sauté pan over high heat. Sprinkle the dry pan with kosher salt then add the remaining 2 tablespoons of the olive oil and wait for it to shimmer, about 30 seconds. Add the leeks and stir until they are soft and translucent, about 5 to 6 minutes. Add the mushrooms and continue cooking until the pan appears dry, about 6 minutes. Remove the pan from the heat and allow the leek mixture to cool.

5 When the leek mixture is cool, add it to the cauliflower. Add the garlic, chives, flaxseed meal, and cheese (if using) to the cauliflower/leek mixture and mix until well combined. Season with salt and pepper to taste.

6 Pour the batter into the greased tins. Bake the muffins for 25 to 30 minutes or until they have browned and begun to pull away from the sides of the muffin tins. Let the muffins cool 10 to 15 minutes before running a paring knife along the inside edges of each muffin tin. Carefully remove each muffin and serve immediately or reheat in a 350°F degree oven for 5 minutes.

MUFFINS ARE GOOD FOR 4 DAYS REFRIGERATED OR 2 MONTHS FROZEN. I RECOMMEND DEFROSTING THE MUFFINS SLOWLY BY PLACING THEM IN THE REFRIGERATOR OVERNIGHT.

BRUSSELS SPROUTS *with* TEMPEH BACON *and* CARAMELIZED SHALLOTS

MAKES 4 SERVINGS

I love Brussels sprouts so much I had to limit myself to two preparations in this book or people might think I own a Brussels sprout farm.

A few years ago I was putting together a fall menu for a large party and my first thought was, "Sautéed Brussels sprout leaves would be a great side here!" My second thought? "Meticulously peeling the leaves off every single sprout is going to be a giant pain and time killer. I'll have to make something else." That's when I discovered chopping them in the food processor—and it changed my life . . . well maybe not, but I make Brussels sprouts this way all the time now and it's awesome.

1½ pounds Brussels sprouts

2 tablespoons extra-virgin olive oil

5 slices tempeh bacon or something similar, chopped

4 medium shallots, sliced crosswise into thin rings

3 garlic cloves, minced

½ cup water

Kosher salt and freshly ground black pepper to taste

1 Remove any unattractive leaves from the outside of the Brussels sprouts and cut each sprout in half. Place half the sprouts in the food processor and pulse until chopped. Do not go ape and turn them into coleslaw; the idea is to just break them up. Stop pulsing when the sprouts are chopped and some of the cores are still intact. Place the chopped sprouts in a medium bowl and repeat the process with the remaining sprouts.

2 Heat a large skillet over high heat. Add the olive oil and wait until it shimmers then add the shallots and stir with a wooden spoon while shaking the pan until the shallots are slightly brown, about 5 minutes. Add the chopped Brussels sprouts and tempeh bacon. Sauté sprouts until they begin to wilt, about 5 minutes; some may start to crisp up or char and that is OK.

3 Add the garlic and water. Continue stirring until the water has completely evaporated, about 3 minutes. (This allows the sprouts to cook evenly and prevents the garlic from burning.)

5 Remove the sprouts from the heat and season them with salt and pepper. Serve immediately.

BRUSSELS SPROUTS ARE GOOD FOR 3 DAYS REFRIGERATED. THEY DO NOT FREEZE WELL.

BALSAMIC-MAPLE ROASTED BRUSSELS SPROUTS

MAKES 4 SERVINGS

This is really the easiest, most delicious side dish ever and once you make this you are armed with the ability to make any number of veggies in the same fashion—just replace the Brussels sprouts with carrots, broccoli, asparagus, sweet potato cubes . . . to name a few. These Brussels sprouts are nature's candy and folks have been known to eat these right from the pan, they are so freakin' good!

1½ pounds Brussels sprouts

3 tablespoons extra-virgin olive oil

4 tablespoons balsamic vinegar

4 tablespoons maple syrup

Kosher salt and freshly ground black pepper to taste

1 Preheat the oven to 450°F.

2 Remove any unattractive leaves from the outside of the Brussels sprouts and cut each sprout in half. In a large bowl toss the sprouts in olive oil, balsamic vinegar, and maple syrup and season with salt and pepper.

3 Place the sprouts on a baking sheet cut side down and roast until caramelized (about 20 minutes). Serve immediately.

BRUSSELS SPROUTS ARE GOOD FOR 3 DAYS REFRIGERATED. THEY DO NOT FREEZE WELL.

SWEET *and* SPICY BAKED BEANS

MAKES 8 SERVINGS

Good ol' baked beans don't get the respect and attention they deserve. They are awesome, kid-friendly, and full of protein. Not to mention they freeze well, which makes them a perfect, no fuss meal on a cold day. I like to top mine with more hot sauce and a little diced raw onion but that's just me. These beans make a great baked potato filling, too.

---

2 tablespoons extra-virgin olive oil

2 medium white or brown onions, diced small

3 red jalapeños, seeded and minced (if red jalapeños are unavailable, use green)

2 green bell peppers, seeded and diced small

One 6-ounce can tomato paste

⅓ cup brown sugar

⅓ cup molasses

1 teaspoon liquid smoke

2 tablespoons hot sauce like Sriracha

1 pound dried navy beans (about 2½ cups), soaked using method 1 or 2 (page 84)

6 cups Better than Bouillon "No Beef" Beef Broth or Rich Dark Vegetable Stock (page 117)

1½ teaspoons+ kosher salt

Freshly ground black pepper as needed

1 Adjust the rack in the oven to accommodate a 6 to 8–quart stockpot or a Dutch oven with a lid then preheat the oven to 325°F.

2 Heat the pot over high heat, add the olive oil, and wait for it to shimmer. Add the onions, jalapeños, and bell pepper and cook until the onions are golden brown (about 10 minutes).

3 Remove the pot from the heat and stir in the tomato paste, sugar, molasses, liquid smoke, hot sauce, soaked beans, and broth. Over medium heat bring the beans to a simmer and stir.

4 Cover the pot snugly, then carefully place it in the oven and bake the beans for 3 hours or until they are tender and the sauce is thick. When the beans are cooked add the salt and pepper.

BEANS ARE GOOD FOR 4 DAYS REFRIGERATED OR 2 MONTHS FROZEN.

> NOTE:
>
> This method calls for oven-baking in a Dutch oven or oven-proof stockpot. This can be done in a crock-pot or over low heat on a stove top but technically they are no longer baked beans. Cooking times will vary but as long as the beans are tender and the liquid is thick it's all good.

SWEET SLAW

MAKES 8 SERVINGS

In addition to my Chickpea Patties (page 198) this slaw goes great with any sandwich or soup. It has a bright, crisp flavor that is a perfect balance to something rich or spicy. Bonus: add some avocado and you have a great a spring roll filling.

---

1 large Napa cabbage, very thinly sliced

2 red jalapeños, seeded and sliced into paper-thin strips (optional)

1 red bell pepper, seeded and sliced into thin strips

½ bunch cilantro, stems included, washed, patted dry, and chopped

3 tablespoons sugar

¼ cup seasoned rice vinegar

2 tablespoons sesame oil

1 bunch scallion, green parts only, sliced as thin as possible

20 big mint leaves, sliced thin

1   In a large bowl combine the cabbage, jalapeño, bell pepper, and cilantro.

2   In a small saucepan stir the sugar, vinegar, and sesame oil over medium heat until the sugar dissolves, about 4 minutes.

3   Remove from heat and pour the warm vinegar mixture over the slaw and toss to coat. Mix in the scallions and mint. Allow the slaw to chill for 20 minutes before serving.

SLAW IS GOOD FOR 2 DAYS REFRIGERATED.

ROSEMARY *and* WHITE BEAN PUREE

Along with the Celeriac alla Florentina (page 173), this aromatic puree works perfectly any time you would normally serve mashed potatoes. It is packed with protein and in my opinion is excellent all by itself.

1 large russet potato, peeled and cut into eighths

Two 15-ounce cans Great Northern or cannellini beans, drained, or 1 cup dried white beans soaked and cooked using method 1 or 2 (page 84). Strain the beans and reserve the cooking liquid to make the broth.

2 tablespoons minced fresh rosemary

1 cup Better than Bouillon "No Chicken" Chicken Broth or Rich Yellow Vegetable Stock (page 116)

Kosher salt and freshly ground black pepper to taste

1 In a small saucepan over medium heat simmer the quartered potato until fork tender. Drain the water and set the potato aside.

2 In a large saucepan heat the beans, rosemary, and broth over medium heat until the mixture comes to a simmer. Smash the beans with a potato masher or the back of a large metal spoon until about three-quarters of the beans are mashed. Stir the bean mixture, then remove it from the heat.

3 Squeeze the cooked potato through a potato ricer or mash it in a small bowl with a fork until smooth. Mix the mashed potato into the beans and season the mixture with salt and pepper. Cover and reserve warm until ready to serve.

BEAN PUREE IS GOOD FOR 4 DAYS REFRIGERATED OR 2 MONTHS FROZEN.

PERFECTLY BAKED YAM FRIES

MAKES 4 SERVINGS

I had a client who liked these fries so much he requested them almost daily. Yams have a long shelf life so it's easy to keep them on hand—you know, for times when you (or someone who depends on you to feed him) HAVE to have yam fries. The key here is a well-preheated hot oven and never overcrowding the fries. I often cook these fries all the way through then combine the two sheet trays and put them aside until the meal is ready, then I reheat the fries in a really hot oven for 3 minutes or so. Try them with the Chipotle Nut Cream on (page 18).

4 medium sweet potatoes, peeled and sliced into just under ¼-inch x ¼-inch fries

1 tablespoon Cajun spice or any spice you prefer (see note)

2 teaspoons cornstarch

Extra-virgin olive oil as needed

Kosher salt and freshly ground black pepper as needed

1 Preheat oven to 450°F.

2 In a large bowl toss the sweet potatoes with the seasoning, cornstarch, and just enough oil to coat. Season with salt and pepper and spread the fries evenly in single layer on two sheet trays.

3 Baking time varies depending on the oven and size of fries but anywhere around 20 minutes is normal. Remove the fries after 10 minutes and turn each one over. Switch the middle fries to the outside and vice-versa. Give the pans a 180-degree turn and switch their positions in the oven. Continue baking until the fries are crisp and soft in the middle, about 10 to 15 minutes. Dark browning is great; the yams are so sweet that they won't taste burnt.

4 Remove trays from the oven and allow the fries to cool slightly before serving; not only are they too hot to eat right out of the oven but they actually get crisper as they cool.

FRIES ARE EDIBLE FOR 3 DAYS REFRIGERATED BUT THEY ARE AT THEIR BEST THE DAY THEY ARE MADE.

NOTE:

Straight, fat potatoes yield the most fries so keep that in mind when selecting. For this recipe you want to buy yams with the deep red skin and orange flesh. I'm trying not to get into the whole yam vs. sweet potato thing but just know that everything available in the United States is a type of sweet potato and that we use the term "yam" to differentiate the red ones from the white ones. Supermarkets compound the problem by labeling them all kinds of things, but historically . . . Oh damn it! . . . JUST GET THE RED ONES!!

NOTE:

I use Cajun spice but any one of Paul Prudhomme's Blackened Spices or your favorite spice blends will work, too, like curry powder, Old Bay, lemon pepper, Spike . . . you can't go wrong.

CLASSIC POTATOES GRATIN

MAKES 6 SERVINGS

While hearty, using cashew cream rather than dairy cream creates a lightness that the traditional recipe just doesn't have. Add fresh herbs and nutmeg? You have a classic side that can do double duty: make it as a treat for your next holiday feast or make it as a comforting side for any weeknight meal.

Vegan butter, as needed for greasing dish

1 batch Cashew Cream (page 16)

½ cup water

4 sprigs fresh thyme

2 tablespoons fresh rosemary leaves, whole

4 garlic cloves, chopped

Big pinch kosher salt and freshly ground black pepper, plus more to taste

½ teaspoon fresh grated nutmeg

3 tablespoons nutritional yeast

2 pounds russet potatoes, peeled and cut into ⅛-inch-thick slices or thinner

1 Preheat the oven to 400°F. Butter a 13 x 9-inch casserole dish with vegan butter.

2 Using a 2 to 3–quart saucepan, bring the Cashew Cream, water, thyme, rosemary, and garlic to a gentle simmer over medium heat. Add salt and pepper and simmer uncovered for 8 minutes. Stir often to prevent scorching. Strain the cream into a small bowl and stir in the nutmeg and nutritional yeast.

3 Slice and rinse the potatoes with hot tap water to remove excess starch. Season the potatoes with salt and pepper.

4 Pour just enough cream into the casserole dish to cover the bottom. Shingle a layer of potatoes in the dish and spoon some cream over the top. Repeat the process until all the potatoes and cream are used. Try to evenly portion out the cream so there's enough for the top layer of potatoes. Shake the dish gently to level out the potatoes.

5 Cover the dish with aluminum foil and poke a few holes to allow steam to escape. Bake for 30 minutes. Uncover and bake an additional 10 minutes. Allow the potatoes to rest about 15 minutes before cutting.

POTATOES ARE GOOD FOR 4 DAYS IN THE FRIDGE OR 2 MONTHS FROZEN. I STRONGLY RECOMMEND CUTTING THE LEFTOVER POTATOES INTO SINGLE PORTIONS BEFORE FREEZING.

NOT YOUR GRAMMY'S GREEN BEAN CASSEROLE

MAKES 6 SERVINGS

Every Thanksgiving I skillfully navigate through a maze of soggy casseroles held together by canned mushroom soup and who knows what from Fritos to canned cream corn. This is a completely fresh version of an old-school classic. Canned basics make way for fresh blanched green beans and porcini mushrooms in a sherry–cashew cream sauce. The topper? Crunchy toasted almonds.

1 ounce dried porcini mushrooms

1 cup sliced almonds

2 tablespoons extra-virgin olive oil

1 pound button mushrooms, thinly sliced

Kosher salt and freshly ground black pepper to taste

1 cup dry sherry

1 batch Cashew Cream (page 16)

2 tablespoons soy sauce

2 pounds fresh green beans, trimmed and washed

1 Rinse mushrooms quickly in cold water to remove excess dirt. Soak them in 1½ cups of hot water until soft (about 10 minutes). Drain the mushrooms and reserve the soaking liquid; let the liquid sit undisturbed.

2 Heat a dry skillet over medium heat and add the almonds, stirring constantly until light brown and toasted (see method on page 125). Set the almonds aside.

3 Heat a large skillet or sauté pan, add the olive oil, and wait for it to shimmer. Add the button mushrooms and cook, stirring often until they are wilted and brown (about 10 minutes). Season the mushrooms with salt and pepper. Add the porcini mushrooms and the top three-quarters of the soaking liquid. Discard remaining soaking liquid and sauté the mushrooms for a few minutes, until the liquid has reduced by more than half.

4 Carefully add the sherry and simmer for 5 minutes or until the liquid has reduced by more than half again. Pour in the Cashew Cream and return it to a simmer for 2 minutes only. Season the creamed 'shrooms with the soy sauce and pepper then remove from the heat, cover, and reserve.

5 Bring a big pot of salted water to a rolling boil. Add the beans and cook for about 5 minutes or until they are just cooked through and bright green. Drain the liquid and arrange the beans in a 9 x 13-inch casserole dish or large platter. Pour the creamed mushrooms over the beans and serve immediately or keep the casserole warm in a 200°F oven until ready to serve. Top with toasted almonds just before serving.

LEFTOVERS ARE GOOD FOR ABOUT 2 DAYS REFRIGERATED. DO NOT FREEZE.

JACKSON'S GREEN BEANS

MAKES 4 SERVINGS

I'm always asked how I get my kids to eat more veggies. My answer is to make them as flavorful as possible and make them again and again. Every day. When it comes to kids you need to make vegetables familiar and common. This is a great basic recipe to get your kids to eat more veg; my son and his friends eat these beans up like crazy. Bonus: this recipe is pretty simple (if my wife can make these perfectly, and cooking is not her thing, trust me . . . so can you).

1 pound green beans, washed and trimmed

2 tablespoons extra-virgin olive oil

¾ cup water

Juice of 1 lemon

Kosher salt and freshly ground black pepper to taste

1 Heat a large stainless steel skillet over high heat and sprinkle it with kosher salt. Add the olive oil and wait for it to shimmer. Add the green beans and toss until char marks appear throughout, about 10 minutes.

2 Carefully add the water and move the beans around while the water simmers and steams. Continue cooking until the water is almost completely gone. Just before serving add the lemon juice and season aggressively with salt and pepper.

THIS IS ONE OF THOSE SIDES THAT IS BEST EATEN THE DAY IT WAS MADE.

BUTTERNUT SQUASH SOUFFLÉ

MAKES 8 SERVINGS

This is not the kind of fussy soufflé that will deflate like an untied balloon if you open the oven door. This is an easy-to-make dish that I generously call a soufflé because it has a light and airy texture. Don't be discouraged if it loses a bit of its dome shape; that's quite okay. Talk about easy—the dish can be completely prepped one day ahead and baked the next day, which makes it perfect for potluck.

½ medium butternut squash
(to yield 2½ cups diced)

1 pound carrots, peeled, chopped,
and steamed or simmered until tender

4 ounces (½ cup) vegan butter, melted

½ cup brown sugar

¾ cup ground flaxseeds or flax meal

½ cup organic flour

3 tablespoons baking powder

1 tablespoon vanilla extract

Salt and freshly ground black pepper to taste

NOTE:

The recipe method calls for individual servings. To serve family style, make one large soufflé in an 8-inch soufflé dish or a casserole dish. Bake at 350°F until set. The cooking time will depend greatly on the size of the dish but 1 hour minimum is a safe bet.

1 Preheat oven to 375°F.

2 Using a serrated knife, halve the squash lengthwise and scoop out the seeds. Place the squash on a sheet tray cut side up and bake for 30 minutes or until the flesh is very tender. Remove the squash from the oven and allow it to cool before scooping out the flesh onto the sheet tray and discarding the skin.

3 Turn the oven up to 450°F.

4 Place the steamed carrots on a sheet tray with the cooked squash and bake the vegetables for about 5 minutes to dry them out a little. Working in batches if necessary, puree the squash and carrot in a food processor until completely smooth. Place the squash mixture in a large mixing bowl and whisk in the remaining ingredients until smooth. Season aggressively with salt and pepper.

5 Fill eight 5-ounce ramekins with an equal amount of the soufflé mixture. These can be made 1 day ahead; cover and refrigerate then bring to room temperature before baking. Bake the soufflés for about 45 minutes or until puffed and a toothpick comes out clean. The soufflés will drop somewhat after cooling.

THE SOUFFLÉS ARE GOOD FOR 3 TO 4 DAYS REFRIGERATED. DO NOT FREEZE.

7 | THE MAIN EVENT

NO-RICE FRIED RICE

MAKES 6+ SERVINGS

I love the flavor of fried rice but I'm not always in the mood for a bowl of carbs. This No-Rice Fried Rice offers the best of both worlds! Using root veggies as "rice," you get a bowl full of goodness with the familiar flavor of fried rice that is suitable as a meal. It reheats well, which makes it a good take-to-work lunch, too.

1 large bulb celeriac

3 large parsnips

2 fat carrots

2 tablespoons extra-virgin olive oil

3 large garlic cloves, minced

1-inch piece fresh ginger, peeled and minced

½ bunch scallions, white and green parts separated and minced

1 cup frozen peas or edamame

2 tablespoons toasted sesame oil

½ cup reduced-sodium soy sauce

1 Peel the celeriac, parsnips, and carrot. Using a box grater or a food processor with the cheese grater attachment, grate the celeriac, parsnips, and carrot and place them in a medium bowl.

2 Heat a large skillet or sauté pan over high heat. Sprinkle the dry pan with salt then add the olive oil and wait for it to shimmer, about 20 seconds. Add the grated vegetables to the pan and stir for about 5 minutes or until the vegetables begin to brown and wilt slightly. Reduce the heat to medium and add the garlic, ginger, and white scallions. Continue cooking for an additional 5 minutes, stirring occasionally.

3 Remove the pan from heat and stir in the peas, sesame oil, soy sauce, and green scallions. Return the pan to medium heat and stir until the mixture is hot. Serve immediately.

NO-RICE FRIED RICE IS GOOD FOR 4 DAYS REFRIGERATED. I DO NOT RECOMMEND FREEZING.

EASY BARLEY *and* FARRO RISOTTO

MAKES 6 SERVINGS

Making traditional risotto is serious business and it takes even a seasoned veteran about 45 minutes of constant attention from start to finish. Barley and farro risotto, on the other hand, is a snap. Cooking the grains may take just as long but this is unattended time, which frees you up to do other things. And, bonus: barley and farro are way better for you than starchy arborio rice. With veggies in the mix here, this is a filling, healthy, and easy dish.

¾ cup farro

¾ cup barley, rinsed

½ cup raw cashews

1½ cups almond milk

2 tablespoons extra-virgin olive oil

3 shallots, minced

3 fresh garlic cloves, minced

1 cup dry white wine or vermouth

1 large zucchini, grated

1 large carrot, peeled, grated, and squeezed dry in paper towels.

1 Rinse and drain the farro. Place it in a medium saucepan with 3 cups of water. Bring the water to a boil; reduce heat to medium-low, and simmer 30 minutes or until tender. Drain any excess water and allow it to cool uncovered.

2 In a small saucepan gently simmer the barley covered in 2¼ cups salted water until tender but chewy (about 20 minutes). Drain any excess water and allow it to cool uncovered. (Although it appears that the grains will be done at the same time, resist the urge to cook the two grains together. The farro will be undercooked.)

3 In another small saucepan bring the cashews to a boil in 2 cups water then remove the pan from the heat and allow the cashews to soak for about 30 minutes then drain and discard the soaking liquid. Using a blender, puree the almond milk and cashews until smooth and set it aside.

4 Heat a large skillet over medium heat then add the olive oil, shallots, and garlic and stir until fragrant (about 2 minutes). Add the wine and simmer until reduced by half, about 5 minutes, then add the zucchini, carrot, and both grains. Toss to incorporate then pour in the nut cream and bring it to a simmer. Season well and continue cooking the risotto until the ingredients are hot, about 5 minutes. Serve immediately.

THE RISOTTO IS GOOD FOR 3 TO 4 DAYS REFRIGERATED. I RECOMMEND ADDING A FEW DASHES OF WATER TO THE RISOTTO WHEN REHEATING, AS THE GRAINS TEND TO SOAK UP A LOT OF LIQUID OVER TIME. I DO NOT SUGGEST FREEZING THIS ONE.

FARRO-STUFFED TOMATOES PROVENÇAL

MAKES 4 SERVINGS

Classically, tomatoes Provençal are not stuffed; they are topped with breadcrumbs and served as a side dish. My version makes these gems more substantial and brings them to the center of the plate. Farro not only has a meaty texture; it is high in protein and has a great nutty flavor.

1½ cups farro

8 firm Roma tomatoes

⅓ cup almond flour

⅓ cup hemp seeds

2 tablespoons extra-virgin olive oil

3 garlic cloves, minced

½ teaspoon kosher salt

1 teaspoon herbes de Provence or ½ teaspoon dried oregano and ½ teaspoon dried thyme

1 tablespoon minced fresh flat-leaf parsley

Kosher salt and freshly ground black pepper to taste

1 Rinse and drain the farro. Place it in a medium saucepan with 3 cups of water. Bring the water to a boil; reduce heat to medium-low, and simmer 30 minutes or until tender. Drain any excess water and discard.

2 Preheat the oven to 375°F.

3 While the farro is cooking, cut the tomatoes in half crosswise and trim the ends just enough so the tomatoes will stand cut side up. Using a melon baller or paring knife, scoop out and discard the insides of the tomato. Pat dry the insides of the tomatoes with a kitchen or paper towel and set them aside.

4 In a medium bowl, mix the cooked farro, almond flour, hemp seeds, olive oil, garlic, salt, herbes de Provence, and parsley. Mix the filling thoroughly and season to taste with salt and pepper.

5 Fill each tomato with the farro mixture. Be sure to push the mixture down into the tomato so that it is really stuffed and full. Place the tomatoes on a foil-lined sheet tray and bake the tomatoes for 20 minutes. Allow the tomatoes to cool slightly before serving.

THE TOMATOES ARE GOOD FOR 4 DAYS REFRIGERATED. THEY DO NOT FREEZE WELL.

GRILLED VEGETABLE LASAGNE
with WILD MUSHROOM SAUCE

MAKES 8 SERVINGS

For some people, lasagne is to buy premade or to throw together to serve a group of hungry (possibly drunk) guys they got suckered into having to feed. This is NOT that type of lasagne. This is really something special . . . it's the kind of dish that people will be begging you to make again! This is for those of us that savor every bite . . . every nuance. . . . The smoky flavors of all the grilled vegetables and the creaminess of the almond ricotta combine with the sexy wild mushroom flavor of the sauce to form a luscious and elegant dish, a dish worthy of an expensive bottle of red wine. Don't waste this on that dude that scarfs up anything you put in front of him in record time.

1 large eggplant, cut crosswise into ¼-inch slices

½ cup extra-virgin olive oil, or as needed for brushing and drizzling

Kosher salt and freshly ground black pepper to taste

2 large zucchini, cut lengthwise into slightly less than ¼-inch slices

2 large yellow squash, cut lengthwise into slightly less than ¼-inch slices

3 fat carrots, peeled and cut lengthwise into ⅛-inch slices

6 portabella mushrooms

2 red onions, halved lengthwise and cut into ¼-inch slices

2 red bell peppers

2 yellow bell peppers

1 batch Wild Mushroom Soup (page 100)

1 box lasagne pasta, cooked according to the package and set aside

1 batch Almond-Tofu Ricotta (page 11)

1 Brush both sides of the eggplant slices with olive oil and season them with salt and pepper, then set them aside on a large plate or sheet tray.

2 In a large bowl toss the zucchini, squash, and carrot slices with a drizzle of oil and season them generously with salt and pepper. Place the seasoned vegetables on the sheet tray with the eggplant and reserve the bowl for the mushrooms.

3 Remove the stems from the portabellas and, using a small teaspoon, scrape off the gills from the underside of the mushrooms then gently peel off the top skin by lightly pinching the overhanging skin and pulling it toward the center of the mushroom. Repeat the process until all of the skin has been removed. Place the peeled mushrooms in the reserved bowl then season the 'shrooms with olive oil, salt, and pepper.

(CONTINUED) >

> (CONTINUED FROM PREVIOUS PAGE)

4 Heat an outdoor grill or grill pan until it is blazing hot. Starting with the eggplant and working in batches, grill all the vegetables until they are soft, charred, and ready to eat. When the grilled mushrooms are cool enough to handle slice them into thin strips and reserve them in a bowl.

5 Toss the sliced red onions in a bowl with 2 tablespoons of olive oil and season them with salt and pepper.

6 Heat a large skillet over high heat until it is blazing hot. Add the onions to the hot skillet and stir frequently until the onions are soft, black, and charred, about 20 minutes. Place the onions in a small bowl and set them aside.

7 Wash and dry the peppers well then place them directly over a high flame, two peppers per burner. (If you don't have a gas stove, see page 33 for other pepper-charring methods.) Turn the peppers with a pair of metal tongs to char all sides. When all surfaces of the peppers are black, place the peppers in a large bowl and cover the bowl to steam the skins. Thinly slice the skinned peppers and place them in a bowl and set them aside.

ASSEMBLY

1 Preheat oven to 350°F and have all your ingredients ready.

2 Lightly grease a large rectangular baking dish, and then spoon about 2 cups of Wild Mushroom Soup onto the bottom of the dish. Cover the sauce with a layer of lasagne pasta then top the pasta with a thin layer of the Tofu-Almond Ricotta (about one-third of the mixture), then a layer of half of the grilled eggplant, then a layer of half of the grilled zucchini, yellow squash, and carrots. Sprinkle on half of the charred onions then half of the roasted red peppers, and half of the sliced mushrooms.

2 Repeat layering the lasagne with 2 cups Wild Mushroom Soup, pasta, another one-third of the Tofu-Almond Ricotta, and the remaining vegetables in the same order then top the vegetables with the remaining third of the Tofu-Almond Ricotta and 2 cups of soup.

3 Cover the dish with foil and bake for 30 minutes or until bubbling hot. Let the lasagne rest about 15 minutes before cutting.

LASAGNE IS GOOD FOR 4 DAYS IN THE FRIDGE OR 2 MONTHS FROZEN. I STRONGLY RECOMMEND CUTTING THE LASAGNE INTO SINGLE PORTIONS BEFORE FREEZING. THIS WAY THE LASAGNE WILL DEFROST FAST AND YOU CAN REMOVE AS FEW PORTIONS AS NEEDED.

EGGPLANT PARM

MAKES 6 SERVINGS

People tend to really enjoy a good eggplant parm. And this is one of those dishes that I truly enjoy making for people even more than I like eating it. Here's the secret to this dish: this eggplant Parmesan is never stacked or baked in sauce so you get to enjoy the contrast of the tomato sauce with the crispy breaded eggplant—no soggy business here. If you're looking for a lighter option, you can season and grill the eggplant instead of breading it but you will want to get dark grill marks to achieve some crispiness.

I sometimes serve this over any grilled green vegetable that is in season, like asparagus or green beans but classically it is served over pasta. I recommend a small mound of capellini or thin linguini seasoned with salt and pepper.

FOR THE ALMOND PARM

½ cup almond flour or ¾ cup sliced almonds ground in a food processor

¼ cup nutritional yeast

1 teaspoon kosher salt

FOR THE EGGPLANT

1 large eggplant cut crosswise into ¼-inch thick slices

Kosher salt and freshly ground black pepper to taste

1 cup nondairy milk (soy, almond, rice, or hemp will work)

¼ cup raw almonds

¾ cup all-purpose flour

4 cups panko breadcrumbs or plain breadcrumbs

¼ cup high-heat oil, like grapeseed or safflower

---

1 batch Basic Tomato Sauce (page 39)

(CONTINUED) >

> (CONTINUED FROM PREVIOUS PAGE)

PREPARE THE ALMOND PARM

1 In a small bowl mix the almond flour, nutritional yeast and salt. Set aside.

PREPARE THE EGGPLANT

1 Line a baking tray with parchment paper and set aside.

2 Lay the eggplant slices out on a cutting board or sheet tray and season generously with salt and pepper. Place the milk and almonds in a blender and puree until smooth. Next, put the flour in a medium bowl. Pour the thickened milk in a shallow baking/pie pan and place the breadcrumbs in another shallow baking/pie pan or in a small sheet tray.

3 Make an assembly line from left to right in the following order: Seasoned eggplant, flour, milk wash, breadcrumbs, then the sheet tray. Dredge one eggplant slice in the flour and shake off excess then dip it in the milk and let the excess drip off, then dredge it in the breadcrumbs until evenly coated. Press both sides down gently with your palms and transfer to the parchment paper-lined sheet tray. Repeat the process until all the slices are breaded. Shingle the eggplant slices if you have to but do not stack.

4 Heat half of the oil in a large skillet (10 to 12 inches) over moderately high heat until it is hot and shimmering but not smoking. Brown the eggplant slices four at a time, turning over once, about 3 minutes per side or until golden brown. Add more oil to the pan as needed to brown all the slices. (Note: Only add oil to an empty pan and allow the oil to heat up before placing eggplant slices in the pan.) Transfer with tongs to paper towels to drain.

ASSEMBLY

1 If you are serving over grilled veggies, place them on each plate. If you are serving with pasta, mound a small amount of plain pasta in the center of the plate.

2 Bank two slices of eggplant on the pasta or veggies per plate and ladle warm tomato sauce over half of the eggplant. Sprinkle the almond parm generously over the top and serve immediately.

EGGPLANT PARM IS GOOD FOR 4 DAYS REFRIGERATED BUT IT WILL NEVER BE AS GOOD AND CRISPY AS THE DAY IT WAS MADE.

GNUDI *("Naked Ravioli")*

MAKES 4 SERVINGS

If you're looking for a fun, delicious homemade pasta, gnudi's your go-to. Gnudi (which means "nude" in Italian) is basically a pasta-free ravioli or "naked ravioli." The key to success here is to be gentle with the gnudi balls—they are easy to make but delicate. Classically, gnudi are full of eggs and cheese, so one of the big advantages of using a vegan recipe is that the gnudi can be tasted and adjusted with seasoning before they are cooked. Frozen spinach is OK here but I prefer to use fresh; whatever you choose be sure to squeeze it dry. Egg replacer is a leavening agent used in egg-free baking. It is available in most supermarkets, health food stores, and online. There are many brands, but my favorite is Ener-G Egg Replacer.

½ block firm tofu

1 teaspoon onion powder

1 teaspoon garlic powder

½ cup nutritional yeast

¼ teaspoon nutmeg, freshly grated if possible

1 teaspoon kosher salt

1 teaspoon freshly ground black pepper

1 pound fresh organic baby spinach (or frozen spinach, thawed)

2 tablespoons egg replacer

½ cup flaxseed meal

¼ cup warm water

⅓ cup semolina flour

1 cup all-purpose or bread flour, plus more for dusting

1 batch Basic Tomato Sauce (page 39) or a really good-quality jarred marinara

1 Cut the tofu into four equal slabs then press the slabs between paper towel–lined kitchen towels until they burst, removing as much liquid as possible. Over a large bowl, push the tofu through a potato ricer or pulse the tofu in a food processor until it is smooth then place the tofu in a large bowl.

2 Using a rubber spatula, fold in the onion powder, garlic powder, yeast, nutmeg, salt, and pepper then set the bowl aside.

3 Mound the fresh spinach in a large skillet and place the skillet over medium heat. It should only take a minute or two for the spinach to start wilting. Turn and stir the spinach until it has completely wilted and liquid is visible in the pan. Remove the pan from the heat and allow the spinach to cool.

4 Line a strong kitchen towel with a paper towel and place the wilted spinach (or thawed frozen spinach) in the center. Bring the corners of the towel together to form a pouch and squeeze as much liquid out of the spinach as possible. (Twist the towel tight and really put some muscle into it!) Roughly chop the spinach and fluff it with your fingers then fold the spinach into the tofu mixture.

5 In a small bowl mix the egg replacer and flaxseed meal with the warm water until well incorporated. Fold the flaxseed meal mixture into the tofu mixture. Fold the semolina flour into the mixture until it is well combined.

6 Dust a parchment paper–lined sheet tray generously with flour and place 1 cup of flour in a small bowl or on a plate. Scoop out a large soup spoon full of the gnudi mixture and shape it into a ball with your palms. (Use a 2-ounce ice-cream scooper instead if you have one.) Roll the ball in flour and place it on the sheet tray. Note: Size and shape really doesn't matter as long as they are all the same. I've seen gnudi made into footballs and dome shapes; they all look great. Repeat the process until all the mixture is used. Cover loosely and let the gnudi rest about 30 minutes in the fridge.

7 In a large pot, bring 4 quarts of generously salted water to a boil. Adjust the heat to maintain a constant but gentle simmer (a raging boil will break the gnudi apart).

8 Carefully slide one-half of the gnudi into the boiling water. Start a 4-minute timer when the gnudi have floated to the top and the water has returned to a simmer. Remove the gnudi using a slotted spoon, place them on a sheet tray or large plate, and cover them loosely to keep them warm while you cook the second batch.

9 Place about four or five gnudi (depending on their size) onto plates or into shallow bowls then spoon a small amount of tomato/marinara sauce over the top. Serve immediately.

THE GNUDI ARE GOOD FOR 3 DAYS REFRIGERATED BUT UNFORTUNATELY THEY DO NOT FREEZE WELL.

NOTE:

If serving with pasta I recommend tossing the pasta in the sauce and serving the gnudi naked atop the pasta.

CELERIAC *alla* FLORENTINA

This classic Italian dish is commonly made with fish but the sweet earthiness of the celeriac works seamlessly. The white bean puree binds the flavors together and turns this dish into a complete meal. For added complexity of flavors I like to serve it over a mound of sautéed spinach. For a 30-minute meal you could make this with your favorite marinara sauce, canned beans, and frozen spinach, but if you have the time it is worth the effort to prepare the meal from scratch.

FOR THE SAUTÉED SPINACH

2 pounds baby spinach leaves

1 tablespoon extra-virgin olive oil

2 medium shallots, sliced thin

Kosher salt and freshly ground black pepper to taste

FOR THE CELERIAC

3 large celeriac bulbs, peeled and rinsed

4 cups Better than Bouillon "No Chicken" Chicken Broth or Rich Yellow Vegetable Stock (page 116)

Kosher salt and freshly ground black pepper to taste

½ cup all-purpose flour

4 tablespoons extra-virgin olive oil

FOR THE TOMATO SAUCE

1 medium white onion, minced or diced small

2 teaspoons dried oregano

6 garlic cloves, chopped

10 Roma tomatoes, using the easy-peel method (page 40) then chopped, or two 14-ounce cans diced tomatoes, strained

1 cup braising liquid

2 tablespoons chopped fresh parsley leaves

2 tablespoons chopped fresh basil leaves

2 tablespoons minced chives or scallion

Kosher salt and freshly ground black pepper to taste

Rosemary and White Bean Puree (page 149)

SPINACH

1 Rinse the spinach in cold water and spin it dry in a salad spinner. If the spinach is really dirty repeat the process until the leaves are really clean.

2 In a large pot, heat the olive oil over medium heat and sauté the shallots for about 2 minutes or until translucent. Add all the spinach and a pinch of salt and pepper. Stir the spinach to incorporate the oil and shallots. Turn the heat up to high and cook the spinach for about 3 minutes, stirring constantly with a wooden spoon until all the spinach is wilted. Season with salt and pepper. Push all the spinach to one side of the pot and position the pot on an uneven surface to allow the liquid to pool away from the spinach (I usually wedge a wooden spoon under the pot). Maintain the spinach warm until assembly.

(CONTINUED) >

> (CONTINUED FROM PREVIOUS PAGE)

CELERIAC AND TOMATO SAUCE

1 Cut each celeriac bulb into roughly two 2½ by 3½-inch rectangles. Save the trimmings for another purpose such as vegetable stock.

2 Place the six pieces of celeriac in a large sauté pan, add enough broth to come three-quarters of the way up the sides of the celeriac. Bring the broth to a simmer and braise the celeriac for about 6 minutes then flip and braise 8 minutes more or until the vegetable is just tender. Remove the celeriac from the broth and place it on a plate to cool. Reserve 1+ cup of the braising liquid for the tomato sauce and discard the rest. When the celeriac is cool enough to handle pat it really dry with paper towels. Season each side with salt and pepper. Dredge each side with flour and shake off any excess.

3 Preheat the oven to warm (150°F to 200°F).

4 Heat a large stainless steel sauté pan or skillet over high heat. Sprinkle the dry pan with kosher salt and shake the pan a bit. Add 2 tablespoons of the olive oil and wait until it shimmers. Cook half the celeriac in the oil until golden brown, about 3 minutes per side. Transfer the browned celeriac to a small foil-lined sheet tray. Add the remaining 2 tablespoons of olive oil to the pan and brown the remaining pieces of celeriac in the same manner. Place the sheet tray of celeriac in the warm oven to retain its heat while you make the sauce.

5 Add the onions to the same pan used for the celeriac and cook until the onions are slightly brown. While the onions are cooking scrape the pan with a wooden spoon to remove any flour bits that may have stuck to the pan from the celeriac. Rub and crush the dry oregano in your palms and add it to the browned onions then add the garlic and stir for about 3 minutes only. Do not allow the garlic to brown.

6 Add the tomatoes and braising liquid and reduce the heat to medium. Simmer the sauce uncovered until it reduces and thickens (about 10 minutes). Stir in the parsley, basil, and chives. Season the sauce with salt and pepper and reserve warm.

ASSEMBLY

1 Warm six dinner plates.

2 Slice each piece of celeriac into ¼-inch slices and reserve.

3 Spoon a medium mound of beans and spinach next to each other on the center of a plate. Ladle about 3 ounces of sauce on each plate and place a warm piece of celeriac over the sauce. Serve immediately.

STORE LEFTOVERS REFRIGERATED IN AN AIRTIGHT CONTAINER. CELERIAC ALLA FLORENTINA IS GOOD FOR 3 DAYS REFRIGERATED.

EVERY DAY IS A GOOD DAY CASSOULET

One of my mentors, Chef Claude Guermont, would insist all of his employees come to work 30 minutes early. We would sit at a large table in the dining room and he would cook for us more often than not . . . cassoulet. He would serve small glasses of red wine and ask questions about our personal life in this charming thick French accent. At the table, Chef made us feel like a family. Then when the meal was finished and the plates all picked up he would fly right into character: yelling, swearing, and being gruff and unpleasant . . . At the end of service this intensity dropped and he would smile. I wanted to be just like him. More than just his cooking was inspiring; he was a true leader, simultaneously ferocious and tender. I loved the man. I really did.

Traditional cassoulet is usually an integration of French leftovers with some sausage and beans added for flavor, so setting out to make it from scratch can be very labor intensive unless you have some duck fat, duck legs, and pork shoulder lying around. Fortunately for us, my vegan version is rather quick and simple.

12 ounces dried white beans (preferably Great Northern), soaked using method 1 or 2 on page 84

8½ cups cold water

2 cups water

1 tablespoon tomato paste

2 field roast "apple sausage" or other good-quality vegan sausage, cut in quarters lengthwise, then cut crosswise into ½-inch pieces

2 field roast "Italian sausage" or other good-quality vegan sausage, cut in quarters lengthwise then cut crosswise into ½-inch pieces

One 6-ounce package organic smoky tempeh strips or smart bacon, minced

6 firm Roma tomatoes, use the easy-peel method (page 40) then dice small, or one 14.5-ounce can diced tomatoes

2 tablespoons extra-virgin olive oil

1 large white onion, diced small

2 celery ribs, minced

6 large garlic cloves, minced

3 fresh thyme sprigs, leaves only, chopped

½ teaspoon kosher salt

½ teaspoon freshly ground black pepper

BREAD CRUMB TOPPING

4 tablespoons extra-virgin olive oil

2½ cups good-quality bread crumbs

2 tablespoons flat-leaf parsley, chopped fine

Kosher salt and freshly ground black pepper as needed

(CONTINUED) >

> (CONTINUED FROM PREVIOUS PAGE)

CASSOULET

1 You will need a 4 to 5–quart casserole dish at least 3 inches deep.

2 Place the soaked beans in a 6 to 8–quart stockpot with 10½ cups cold water and the tomato paste then bring the beans to a boil. Reduce the heat to a gentle simmer. Simmer the beans uncovered, until they are almost tender, about 45 minutes to 1 hour. Stir in the sausage, tempeh, and tomatoes and simmer until beans are completely tender, about 15 minutes more.

3 Heat a large skillet or sauté pan over high heat. Add the olive oil and wait until it shimmers. Add the onions and stir or agitate the pan until the onions are golden brown (about 8 minutes). Stir in the celery and cook 2 minutes more. Add the garlic, thyme, salt, and pepper and stir.

4 Add the onion mixture to the cooked beans and gently stir until well combined.

5 Preheat oven to 350°F.

BREAD CRUMB TOPPING

1 In a large skillet or sauté pan heat the olive oil over medium heat. Add the bread crumbs to the oil and stir until they are a light golden brown, about 2 minutes.

2 Remove the bread crumbs from the heat and stir in the parsley and season aggressively with salt and pepper.

ASSEMBLY

1 Ladle the cassoulet into the casserole dish. The beans should be level with liquid; if they are submerged, ladle excess liquid back into the pot and boil it until reduced, then pour it back into the casserole dish.

2 Spread the bread crumb topping evenly over the cassoulet and bake, uncovered, until bubbling and the crust is golden, 20 to 25 minutes. Let the cassoulet rest about 15 minutes before serving.

LEFTOVERS ARE GOOD FOR 4 DAYS REFRIGERATED OR UP TO 2 MONTHS FROZEN.

BEEFLESS BOURGUIGNON

MAKES 6 SERVINGS

Most folks don't think of vegan dishes as having the rich, silky flavors of reduced red wine and broth, but then again most folks don't know how delicious vegan food can really be.

This is definitely the dish to serve to your non-vegan friends when they come over for dinner. If you really want to knock their socks off, start with a simple salad of Boston lettuce, balsamic vinaigrette, and pecans, then move on to some crusty French bread and Earth Balance butter with this Beefless Bourguignon. They won't know what to do with themselves.

Three 9-ounce bags Gardein Beefless Tips

Freshly ground black pepper to taste

3 tablespoons extra-virgin olive oil

2 large brown onions, thinly sliced

4 garlic cloves, minced

¼ cup all-purpose flour

One 750-ml bottle of red burgundy or pinot noir

3 cups *Better than Bouillon* "No Beef" Beef Broth or Rich Dark Vegetable Stock (page 117)

1 pound button mushrooms, washed, dried, and quartered

1 tablespoon chopped fresh thyme

2 tablespoons chopped flat-leaf parsley

1 tablespoon chopped fresh rosemary

4 medium white potatoes, peeled and diced large

6 carrots, peeled and cut into 1-inch pieces

Kosher salt to taste

1 Defrost the beefless tips and season with pepper. Set aside.

2 Heat a heavy-bottom 8-quart stockpot over high heat. Sprinkle the dry pan with kosher salt then add the 3 tablespoons of olive oil and wait for it to shimmer. Add the onions and stir until golden brown (about 12 minutes). Add the garlic and stir for just 1 minute. Sprinkle the flour over the onions and garlic and stir it in. Continue to cook over high heat for about 4 to 5 minutes, stirring often.

3 Pour in the entire bottle of wine, the broth, and the beefless tips. Using a wooden spoon, scrape up all that really good stuff stuck to the bottom of the pot. Add the mushrooms to the pot and adjust the heat to maintain the liquid at a gentle simmer. Stir in the thyme, parsley, and rosemary and let the liquid reduce and thicken.

NOTE:

If you prefer, you can substitute the Gardein beefless tips with 1½ pounds of broccoli florets. Add the broccoli at the end, a few minutes after the carrots.

4   At first the sauce will be purple and watery; after about 20 minutes it will be brown and silky. At this point add the potatoes and 5 minutes later add the carrots. Continue simmering at low heat until the potatoes are tender, about 12 minutes. Scrape the bottom of the pot once in a while to make sure nothing is sticking. At the last minute season the stew with salt and pepper if needed and serve a generous portion into each of 6 bowls. Try to get an even amount of vegetables, tips, and sauce in each bowl.

STORE ANY LEFTOVERS IN AN AIRTIGHT CONTAINER AND REFRIGERATE. BOURGUIGNON IS GOOD FOR 4 DAYS REFRIGERATED OR 2 MONTHS FROZEN.

TIP:

For this recipe, pretend you're on a cooking show. I strongly recommend prepping everything you need ahead of time then follow the directions in order. This will be faster in the long run and it will avoid unnecessary stopping and restarting.

BLANQUETTE *de* LEGUMES

A blanquette is a classic French stew prepared without browning any of the ingredients and most typically made with veal. I know . . . I know . . . but my attitude here is to embrace the technique. It's the basic ingredients and technique that produce the flavors, not the meat. I especially like this version because it is a hearty one-pot meal that is easy to make, filling, and (considering its origins) unexpected from vegan cooks.

---

5 tablespoons vegan butter or extra-virgin olive oil

2 white onions, diced medium

6 celery ribs cut into ¼-inch pieces

¾ cup all-purpose flour

6 garlic cloves, minced

6 cups Better than Bouillon "No Chicken" Chicken Broth or Rich Yellow Vegetable Stock (page 116)

2 cups almond milk

2 pounds small white button mushrooms, washed, patted dry, and quartered lengthwise

2 tablespoons chopped fresh thyme, plus several sprigs for garnish

3 medium white or golden potatoes, peeled and cut into ½-inch cubes

2 carrots, peeled and cut into ½-inch pieces

3 medium zucchinis, peeled, quartered lengthwise, and cut into ½-inch pieces

Kosher salt and freshly ground black pepper to taste

---

1 pound linguine or 6 cups steamed white rice

1 tablespoon fresh parsley, chopped very small

1 Heat a heavy-bottom 8-quart stockpot over medium heat.

2 Sprinkle the dry pan with kosher salt then add the butter. Add the onions and celery and stir until translucent (soft but with *no color*), about 8 minutes. Reduce the heat to low and sprinkle in the flour ¼ cup at a time, stirring in between each addition. Add the garlic and stir for just 1 minute. Add the broth and almond milk then turn the heat up to high and bring the liquid to a simmer. Use a flat-tipped wooden spoon rub the bottom of the pot to release any onion or flour that might be stuck. (In this dish color is the enemy so you want to avoid any situation that could lead to browning).

3 Add the mushrooms and thyme to the pot and adjust the heat to maintain the liquid at a gentle simmer. Simmer uncovered until the liquid has reduced and thickened slightly (about 15 minutes).

4 Rub the bottom of the pot again then add the potatoes and wait 5 minutes before adding the carrots. Simmer the carrots for 5 minutes then add the zucchini. After 5 minutes more the potatoes, carrots, and zucchini should be cooked perfectly. Remove the blanquette from the heat. Season with salt and pepper and cover until ready to serve.

ASSEMBLY

1 Using large shallow bowls, mound a serving of pasta in the center of each bowl and ladle a healthy amount of the blanquette over the top, ensuring an even variety of vegetables on every plate. Garnish with parsley and thyme sprigs.

REFRIGERATE ANY UNUSED PORTION OF THE BLANQUETTE. THE STEW IS GOOD FOR 4 DAYS IN THE FRIDGE AND 2 MONTHS IN THE FREEZER.

RATATOUILLE

MAKES 6 SERVINGS

Proper ratatouille is not a side dish. It is undoubtedly a meal. There is a lot of protein in all these vegetables and it has so many flavor complexities that there really is no room for an accompaniment.

I take the preparation of ratatouille seriously because I can see how someone might look at the final product and assume that dumping all the ingredients in a pot and cooking them until they are soft is how it is made. (That approach would produce horrible ratatouille!) You have to treat each ingredient as an important gear in a complex clock. That being said, the absence of one yellow squash or one red pepper isn't something to get hung up on; it is more about how your ingredients are treated that makes a difference.

For this recipe I insist you prep everything you need ahead of time, chopping all the vegetables and herbs and keeping them separate, then follow the directions in order. At first you will probably want to hunt me down and punch me in the face, but by the end of the recipe you will want to hug me . . . I promise.

¼ cup extra-virgin olive oil, as needed

1 medium white or brown onion, diced small

1 medium red onion, diced small

3 celery ribs, cut in half lengthwise then sliced very thin crosswise

12 ounces small to medium button mushrooms, quartered lengthwise

Kosher salt and freshly ground black pepper to taste

1 medium eggplant (not Japanese), diced small

1 yellow bell pepper, seeded and diced small

1 red bell pepper, seeded and diced small

2 fat carrots peeled, quartered lengthwise, and sliced thin

2 zucchinis, quartered lengthwise and cut crosswise into ¼-inch pieces

2 yellow squash, quartered lengthwise and cut crosswise into ¼-inch pieces

6 firm Roma tomatoes, use the easy-peel method (page 40) then dice, or one 14-ounce can diced tomatoes, drained

6 large garlic cloves, minced

½ bunch parsley, chopped

10 large fresh basil leaves, chopped

4 thyme sprigs, leaves only, chopped

(CONTINUED) >

> (CONTINUED FROM PREVIOUS PAGE)

1 Heat a large stainless steel skillet or 10-inch fry pan over high heat and sprinkle it with kosher salt. Add about 2 tablespoons of the olive oil and wait for it to shimmer, then add the onions and stir them occasionally until they are wilted and lightly caramelized, about 12 minutes. Add the celery to the onions and continue cooking for a few minutes longer. Using a heatproof rubber spatula or a wooden spoon, dump the onions into a small stockpot. *Do not heat the stockpot yet.*

2 Carefully wipe the skillet with a paper towel and return it to the heat, drizzle in some more oil, and wait for it to shimmer. Add the mushrooms and cook until they release their juices and brown slightly, about 8 minutes. Season the mushrooms with salt and pepper and add them to the stockpot.

3 Wipe the pan clean again and return it to the heat, drizzle in some more oil and wait for it to shimmer. Add the eggplant and stir or agitate the pan constantly. Cook and season the eggplant with salt and pepper until it is wilted and shows some color (about 10 minutes). Add the eggplant to the stockpot, and this time wash the pan and dry it really well.

4 Heat the pan over high heat, drizzle in some oil, and wait for the shimmer. *(By now you're a pro).* Add the bell peppers and stir or agitate the pan constantly. Cook the peppers until they char slightly (about 5 minutes). Add the peppers to the stockpot, wipe the pan clean, return it to the heat and drizzle in some oil. When it shimmers add the carrots and cook about 2 minutes then add the zucchini and squash and cook until slightly browned (5 to 8 minutes). Add the carrot mixture to the stockpot.

5 Place the stockpot over medium heat and mix the ingredients gently until well combined. Stir in the chopped tomatoes and garlic and cook until the ratatouille is hot, taste and season the stew well with salt and pepper. Stir in all the herbs, cover, and remove from the heat. At this point the ratatouille can be served or reserved off the heat until needed. If not eaten immediately, reheat over medium-low heat and serve. (Do not leave it at a simmer if you are not ready to eat; the vegetables will be mushy and all your hard work will be pointless).

RATATOUILLE IS GOOD FOR 4 DAYS. I DO NOT RECOMMEND FREEZING.

LEMON HERB BARLEY SUMMER VEG PLATTER

MAKES 10 SERVINGS

This delicious and attractive platter really highlights what eating a balanced vegan diet is all about. Serve this alone or with a simple salad of mixed greens and spinach or my Best Kale Salad Ever (page 120) for an awesome meal. Have leftovers? Stuff those grilled veggies between some bread and slap on some Basic Mayo or Wasabi Aioli (pages 36, 35) for a great cold sandwich and serve with a side of lemon barley.

LEMON BARLEY

2 cups dried barley

5 cups water

3 tablespoons Garlic Oil (page 54)

1 teaspoon Dijon mustard

Zest of 1 lemon

Juice of 1 lemon

¼ cup flaxseed

¼ cup chives, sliced very thin

10 large basil leaves, chopped fine

1 fresh rosemary sprig, leaves only, minced

Kosher salt and freshly ground black pepper to taste

GRILLED VEGETABLES

4 portabella mushrooms, stems and top skin removed, gills scraped off with a spoon

Garlic Oil (page 54) as needed

Kosher salt and freshly ground black pepper to taste

1 bunch asparagus, tough ends removed

2 red bell peppers, quartered lengthwise and seeds removed

2 medium zucchinis, cut diagonally into ¼-inch thick slices

2 yellow squash, cut diagonally into ¼-inch thick slices

1 eggplant, cut into ¼-inch thick rounds

(CONTINUED) >

LEMON BARLEY

1 Rinse the barley in cold water.

2 In a large saucepan bring the water and barley to a simmer over high heat. Cover and reduce the heat to low. Cook the barley until tender but not mushy, about 25 minutes. Drain any excess liquid and allow the barley to cool.

3 While the barley is cooking whisk the Garlic Oil, mustard, lemon zest, and lemon juice in a medium bowl.

4 In a large bowl combine the barley, vinaigrette, flaxseed, and herbs. Season with salt and pepper. Cover and reserve at room temperature.

VEGETABLES

1 Cut the portabellas into ½-inch strips.

2 In a medium bowl toss the mushrooms gently with a drizzle of Garlic Oil and season with salt and pepper. Mound the mushrooms on a foil-lined sheet tray, leaving room for the other ingredients. Using the same bowl repeat the process with the remaining vegetables. Be sure to maintain the vegetables separately.

3 Heat an outdoor grill and be aware of your grill's hot spots. Using metal tongs grill the vegetables 1 or 2 varieties at a time, turning and flipping as necessary. Be sure to grill the eggplant until it is charred and floppy.

4 Arrange the grilled vegetables on a large platter and arrange the barley salad next to the grilled vegetables. Serve immediately or cover loosely and hold warm until needed.

BARLEY AND GRILLED VEG ARE GOOD FOR 4 DAYS REFRIGERATED.

BRAISED DAIKON SCALLOPS *with* SUGAR SNAP PEAS *and* SHIITAKE

MAKES 6 SERVINGS

Daikon is amazingly good for your kidneys and circulatory system, but what's really cool about it is its structure. It is crisp like a jicama but with a strong radish flavor. When cooked it takes on a firm, meaty texture. I like to braise it with sweet liquids to balance the peppery spice of the radish.

Sake in my opinion comes in two forms: really good and really cheap. I drink good sake and cook with cheap sake and, no, they are never one and the same. If cheap sake is unavailable, any Pinot Grigio will work. Aji-mirin is a cooking wine that is like sake but sweeter. Most supermarkets carry aji-mirin but if you have trouble finding it, an Asian market will have it for sure.

FOR THE DAIKON

2 cups sake

¼ cup good-quality soy sauce

½ cup aji-mirin

3 tablespoons white miso

3 tablespoons brown sugar

6 garlic cloves, crushed

1 tablespoon black peppercorns

3 large daikon radishes, peeled and cut into 1-inch-thick disks

1 teaspoon Sriracha

2 tablespoons sesame oil

2 tablespoons No-Fuss Ketchup (page 38), or store-bought vegan ketchup

1 tablespoon cornstarch plus ¼ cup water

FOR THE VEGETABLES

2 tablespoons grapeseed or safflower oil

1 red bell pepper, seeded and julienned

1½ pounds sugar snap peas, stems and strings removed

10 ounces chopped shiitake mushrooms, cut in half and stems removed

4 garlic cloves, minced

2 tablespoons grated fresh ginger

1 bunch scallions, white and green parts, sliced thin

½ cup Better than Bouillon "No Chicken" Chicken Broth or Rich Yellow Vegetable Stock (page 116)

2 tablespoons reduced-sodium soy sauce

2 tablespoons white or black sesame seeds

(CONTINUED) >

DAIKON

1 Line a plate with paper towels.

2 In a 3-quart sauté pan, stir the sake, soy sauce, aji-mirin, miso, sugar, garlic, and peppercorns. Add the daikon and bring the liquid to a gentle simmer. Simmer the daikon uncovered for 45 minutes. Remove the daikon and reserve them on the towel-lined plate.

3 Stir the Sriracha, sesame oil, and ketchup into the braising liquid.

4 In a small bowl stir together the cornstarch and water to make a slurry. With the braising liquid at a simmer, whisk in the slurry. The sauce should stop simmering for a minute; continue whisking until the liquid returns to a simmer. Allow the sauce to simmer for about 5 minutes then strain the sauce into a small saucepan and reserve.

VEGETABLES

1 While the daikon is braising prepare the rest of the vegetables. Heat a very large sauté pan over high heat. Add half the oil and wait until it shimmers. Add the bell peppers into the hot pan and toss. Continue cooking the peppers until they are wilted and show signs of charring, about 10 minutes. Place the peppers in a small bowl and reserve.

2 Add the remaining tablespoon of oil to the hot pan and add the peas. Cook the peas for 3 minutes then add the mushrooms, garlic, ginger, and scallions and cook an additional 3 minutes.

3 Add the broth and soy sauce and simmer until the liquid reduces (about 5 minutes). Stir in the bell peppers and the sesame seeds, then remove the pan from the heat.

ASSEMBLY

1 Heat a medium skillet with a drizzle of oil. Place the daikon disks in the pan and sear until golden brown on one side then flip and sear on the other side (about 1 minute per side).

2 Mound about ⅙th of the mushroom mixture in the center of a large plate and spoon a bit of sauce from the pan over the top. Place three braised daikon disks around the veg and drizzle each one with the braising liquid sauce. Serve immediately.

STORED SEPARATELY, THIS DISH IS GOOD FOR 3 DAYS, WHILE THE BRAISED DAIKON ALONE IS GOOD FOR 1 WEEK.

MISO-MARINATED PORTABELLA
and EGGPLANT *over* SOBA NOODLES

MAKES 4 SERVINGS

Using a portabella mushroom in a vegan dish is considered "unimaginative" or way too "cliché," and generally speaking, I'm inclined to agree, but here's the thing . . . portabellas are rad! They taste unbelievably good when marinated and really hold any flavor you give them. Paired with eggplant, broccoli, and soba, they make for a dish I would be proud to put on a restaurant menu. So if you are a "foodie" or some gnarly vegan cookbook critic ready to blast me for using the portabella, "Go suck a bag of lemons!!"

FOR THE MARINADE

¼ cup sake

¼ cup aji-mirin

½ cup white miso paste

¼ cup organic brown sugar

4 large garlic cloves, grated on a microplane zester or finely minced

One 1-inch piece ginger, peeled and grated on a microplane zester or finely minced

Zest of 1 tangerine (if available) or ½ orange

Juice of 1 tangerine (if available) or ½ orange

Freshly ground black pepper as needed

NOTE:

You should plan to marinate the veggies for at least three hours.

FOR THE NOODLES

One 9.5-ounce package organic soba noodles

1 tablespoon dark sesame oil

1 tablespoon extra-virgin olive oil

1 large red or yellow bell pepper, sliced thin

1 bunch scallions, sliced very thin on the bias, white and green parts held separately

1 pound (4 cups) broccoli, cut into small, bite-size florets

¼ cup reduced-sodium soy sauce

4 large, thick portabella mushrooms

4 medium Japanese eggplants, trimmed and halved lengthwise

MARINADE

1 In a small saucepan over medium heat, simmer and whisk the sake, aji-mirin, miso, and sugar until the sugar is dissolved and the alcohol is cooked out of the sake, about 5 minutes. Remove the pan from the heat and stir in the garlic, ginger, zest, and juice. Grind in some pepper to taste.

MUSHROOMS

1 For each mushroom, remove the stem, and using a small teaspoon, scrape off the gills. Gently peel the top skin from the mushroom to allow the marinade to penetrate the flesh. In a large bowl gently mix the mushrooms and eggplant in the marinade so that all sides are generously coated.

(CONTINUED) >

> (CONTINUED FROM PREVIOUS PAGE)

2 Cover and refrigerate for at least 3 hours and up to 1 day.

SOBA NOODLES

1 Cook the noodles according to the directions on the package. Drain and reserve the noodles in a large metal bowl. Add the sesame oil to the noodles and toss to coat and prevent sticking.

2 Heat a large sauté pan or skillet over high heat until it is blazing hot. Sprinkle the dry pan with a dash of kosher salt. Add the olive oil and wait for it to shimmer. Add the peppers and toss until they are soft and charred, about 8 to 10 minutes. Just before the peppers look done stir in the white scallions and toss until the onions look wilted, about 2 minutes. Add the peppers and onions to the soba noodles and mix in the green scallions as well.

3 In a large stockpot bring about 3 quarts of water and a pinch of salt to a rolling boil.

4 Add the broccoli florets to the boiling water and cook them until they turn bright green but not soft (about 3 minutes). Remove the broccoli with a spider skimmer, strainer, or slotted spoon, keeping the hot water in the pot. Add the broccoli florets and soy sauce to the soba noodles.

ASSEMBLY

1 Bring the mushrooms and eggplant to room temp.

2 Preheat the oven to 450°F. Lightly oil a foil-lined sheet tray and place the mushroom and eggplant flat side up on the sheet tray.

3 Bring the broccoli water back to a boil.

4 Bake the mushrooms and eggplants for 9 minutes. While the mushrooms are in the oven heat the soba noodles by placing the bowl over the boiling water and gently tossing the noodles.

5 Using a pair of tongs, mound a generous portion of noodles in a shallow bowl or large plate. Place one mushroom and two eggplant halves over the noodles and spoon a little extra marinade over the veg. Serve immediately.

THIS DISH DOES NOT FREEZE WELL BUT IS GOOD FOR 3 TO 4 DAYS IN THE FRIDGE.

UMAMI PATTIES *with* SHIITAKE *and* PEPPERS

MAKES 6 SERVINGS

Umami is one of the five flavor profiles that humans can detect on their tongue. Difficult to describe, it is somewhere between a mushroom–tomato flavor. Umami accentuates flavors the way salt does. If you're still not quite sure what the umami buzz is about, just make these patties and get your umami on!

---

1 pound fresh shiitake mushrooms, with stems, washed and patted dry

2 cups raw walnut pieces

2 garlic cloves, minced

2 tablespoons balsamic vinegar

2 tablespoons vegan Worcestershire sauce

1 bunch scallions, sliced thin, green and white parts held separately

½ cup red quinoa (or whatever is available), rinsed and cooked in 1 cup water until tender

Kosher salt and freshly ground black pepper

2 tablespoons extra-virgin olive oil

1 red bell pepper, seeded and sliced in thin strips

1 yellow bell pepper, seeded and sliced in thin strips

2 teaspoons reduced-sodium soy sauce

½ teaspoon sesame oil

High-heat oil, like grapeseed or safflower as needed

1 Remove and chop the stems from the shiitakes and set them aside. Cut the shiitake caps in half then slice them as thin as possible crosswise and reserve. In a food processor pulse the chopped mushroom stems with the walnuts, garlic, balsamic, and Worcestershire until the mixture is finely ground and clumpy. Add the green scallions and quinoa and pulse a few times until well incorporated.

2 Place the quinoa mixture in a medium bowl and season with salt and pepper then cover and refrigerate for 20 minutes to firm up.

3 Heat a large skillet or sauté pan over high heat then add the olive oil and wait for it to shimmer. Add the bell peppers to the pan and stir until they are soft and slightly charred. Add the sliced mushrooms to the pan and stir until they are wilted and fragrant, about 5 minutes.

4 Remove the pan from the heat and immediately add the white scallions, toss the vegetables, then drizzle in the soy sauce and sesame oil, toss again and put aside until assembly.

5 Remove the quinoa nut mixture from fridge and shape it into ¼-cup patties. Heat a skillet or sauté pan over medium heat and add a drizzle of high-heat oil and wait until it shimmers. Gingerly place half the patties in the pan and cook them about 3 minutes per side or until dark golden brown. (Try to flip each patty only once.) Place the cooked patties on a large plate or sheet tray. Cook the remaining patties in the same fashion.

ASSEMBLY

1 Just before the patties are fully cooked reheat the peppers and mushrooms, then mound some of this mixture in the center of a plate, top it with two patties, and serve.

PATTIES ARE GOOD UP TO 4 DAYS IN THE REFRIGERATOR OR 2 MONTHS FROZEN.

COCONUT CURRY SQUASH STEW

MAKES 6 SERVINGS

For my family good Thai food is our idea of fast food. Our order is always the same—and hey, they deliver. But here's the thing: it's not as mystical as you might think and when you have the time it is so much better made at home. I recommend this dish with a scoop of brown or jasmine rice but it is quite good on its own, too. For a different experience substitute cauliflower, broccoli, or yellow potatoes for the squash. No matter if you follow the recipe below or customize it, flavorful, rich, and satisfying are just three words to describe this stew. Amazing, amazing, and amazing are three more.

3 tablespoons extra-virgin olive oil

½ teaspoon chili flakes (optional)

2 medium white onions, diced medium

4 celery stalks cut crosswise into ¼-inch pieces

4 garlic cloves, minced

One 1-inch piece ginger, peeled and minced

2 tablespoons tomato paste

3 tablespoons Curry Powder (page 57) or store bought

1 cinnamon stick

2 cups Better than Bouillon "No Chicken" Chicken Broth or Rich Yellow Vegetable Stock (page 116)

Two 15-ounce cans organic Thai coconut milk

2 pounds kabocha or butternut squash, peeled and cut into 1-inch pieces (about 2 kabocha or 1 large butternut squash)

1 large red or yellow bell pepper, diced large

½ bunch cilantro, stems included, chopped

12 large fresh mint leaves, chopped

½ bunch scallions, green parts only, sliced thin on the bias

Juice of 1 lime

Kosher salt and freshly ground black pepper

6 cups steamed white or brown rice, for serving

1 Heat a heavy-bottom 8-quart stockpot over high heat. Sprinkle the dry pan with kosher salt then add the olive oil and wait for it to shimmer. Add the chili flakes (if using) and onions and stir until golden brown (about 12 minutes). Add the celery, garlic, and ginger and stir a few minutes more. Stir in the tomato paste, curry powder, and cinnamon stick until combined. Pour in the broth and coconut milk and bring it to a simmer.

2 Immediately stir in the squash and bell pepper and simmer the stew for about 15 minutes or until the squash is tender. Be sure to stir the stew, scraping the bottom of the pot once in a while to make sure nothing is sticking.

3 When the squash is tender stir in the cilantro, mint, scallions, and lime juice. Season aggressively with salt and pepper. Serve immediately over rice. Store any leftovers in an airtight container and refrigerate.

STEW IS GOOD FOR 5 DAYS REFRIGERATED OR 2 MONTHS FROZEN ALTHOUGH THE SQUASH WILL GET A LITTLE MUSHY IN THE PROCESS. AS WITH ANYTHING, I RECOMMEND FREEZING THE STEW THIN AND FLAT IN A RESEALABLE PLASTIC BAG. WHEN THE STEW IS FROZEN SOLID IT CAN BE STACKED NEATLY IN THE FREEZER. THIS MAKES DEFROSTING FAST AND EASY.

ASIAN-STYLE MARINATED CHICKPEA PATTIES *with* SWEET SLAW

MAKES 8 SERVINGS (1 PATTY PER PERSON)

Have you ever been to a street fair or Mongolian BBQ place and been entranced by the wafting aroma of some sort of grilled Asian sweetness? Well this is THAT! Packed with protein and full of flavor, these patties have that sweet essence previously enjoyed only by folks chomping on meat on a stick.

1 batch Sweet Slaw (page 148)

2 cups dried chickpeas, soaked and cooked until tender (see page 84) or two 14-ounce cans drained

¼ cup all-purpose flour

¼ cup soy sauce

2 tablespoons balsamic vinegar

2 tablespoons brown sugar

2 tablespoons minced fresh ginger

3 garlic cloves, minced

¾ cup flaxseed meal

2 large carrots, peeled and grated

Kosher salt and freshly ground black pepper to taste

1 Prepare the slaw and set aside in the fridge to chill.

2 In a food processor combine the chickpeas, flour, soy sauce, vinegar, sugar, ginger, and garlic and pulse a few times until the mixture is combined and chunky—it should *not* be smooth.

3 In a large bowl mix the chickpea mixture with the flaxseed meal and carrots. Taste the mixture and season with salt and pepper accordingly. Scoop a half-cup of mixture and shape it into a patty. The mixture should make eight patties. Place the patties on a sheet tray or in a casserole dish, cover with plastic wrap, and let them rest/marinate in the fridge for 30 minutes to 1 day.

4 Heat an outdoor BBQ, a grill pan, or cast-iron skillet over high heat. Spray the outdoor grill with nonstick spray or drizzle the grill pan or skillet with extra-virgin olive oil. Grill the patties about 3 minutes per side. Use a strong metal spatula to gently flip the patties. Serve the patties over a bed of the Sweet Slaw.

PATTIES ARE GOOD FOR 4 DAYS REFRIGERATED OR 2 MONTHS FROZEN.

BAINGAN BHARTHA

MAKES 4 SERVINGS

Smoky, earthy, and warm, this Indian stew is perfect for sharing family style with people you love (or even ones you just like fine). You can serve this with jasmine rice, but if you want to go for broke, go ahead and eat this on flatbread with your hands. I'm usually not a white wine guy but a chilled Riesling goes great here.

---

2 medium eggplants (just under 2 pounds)

¼ cup extra-virgin olive oil or as needed

Kosher salt to taste

1 large white onion, diced small

6 garlic cloves, minced

Two 1-inch pieces ginger, peeled and minced

6 firm Roma tomatoes, chopped in a food processor until almost smooth

2 teaspoons ground cumin

2 teaspoons turmeric

2 teaspoons chili powder

2 teaspoons cinnamon

Freshly ground black pepper to taste

½ bunch cilantro, stems included, chopped

1 Slice the eggplants into ½-inch slices, brush both sides lightly with olive oil, and season with kosher salt.

2 Heat a grill pan or outdoor grill until it is blazing hot. Working in batches, grill the eggplant until dark and charred on both sides then set them aside to cool. (This can also be done in a cast-iron skillet if necessary.) Chop the eggplant pieces in quarters and set them aside until needed.

3 Heat a large skillet or sauté pan over high heat then add a drizzle of oil and wait for it to shimmer. Add the onion and stir until golden brown (about 12 minutes) then add the garlic and ginger and cook for 2 minutes more.

4 Reduce the heat to medium-low and pour in the chopped tomatoes and bring the mixture to a simmer. Add the eggplant then stir in all the spices and allow the sauce to reduce until it is no longer watery, about 5 minutes. It should have a thick, pulpy texture.

5 Season with salt and pepper then place the Baingan Bhartha in a large serving dish and top with fresh chopped cilantro. Serve hot with jasmine rice and plenty of lavash or any kind of flatbread.

STORE ANY LEFTOVERS IN AN AIRTIGHT CONTAINER AND REFRIGERATE. STEW IS GOOD FOR 4 DAYS REFRIGERATED OR 2 MONTHS FROZEN.

QUINOA MOUSSAKA

MAKES 6 SERVINGS

Quinoa is an awesome source of balanced protein, carbohydrates, and fiber. It has become the go-to grain staple for vegans and nonvegans alike. In this recipe, I recommend red quinoa because it has a nuttier flavor and its dark color looks best in this dish, but feel free to use whatever is available. Moussaka is a classic Greek casserole, generally consisting of vegetables, ground meat, and topped with yogurt. Here, all of the familiar flavor profiles are kicking, leaving you feeling Moussaka-fied, but not stuffed and bloated.

FOR THE BASE

1 large eggplant, sliced crosswise into ¼-inch slices

Extra-virgin olive oil as needed for grilling the eggplant

¾ cup red quinoa, rinsed

1½ cups cool water

4 fat carrots, peeled and grated thick on a box grater or with a food processor attachment

Kosher salt and freshly ground black pepper to taste

FOR THE SAUCE

2 tablespoons extra-virgin olive oil

1 large white onion, diced small

4 garlic cloves, minced

½ cup water

10 firm plum or Roma tomatoes, peeled (see page 40) and chopped

2 teaspoons cinnamon

2 teaspoons dried oregano

¼ teaspoon nutmeg

¼ teaspoon ground clove

Kosher salt and freshly ground black pepper to taste

FOR THE TOPPING

½ cup raw cashews

1½ cups almond milk

1 block firm tofu

2 ounces (¼ cup) vegan butter

¼ cup all-purpose flour

1 pinch finely grated nutmeg

1 teaspoon kosher salt

½ teaspoon freshly ground black pepper

1 tablespoon nutritional yeast

BASE

1 Brush both sides of the eggplant slices with olive oil and season them with salt and pepper, then set them aside on a sheet tray.

2 Heat an outdoor grill or grill pan until it is blazing hot. Grill both sides of the eggplant until charred but slightly undercooked, about 2 minutes per side.

3 Heat a dry saucepan over high heat then sprinkle a pinch of kosher salt in the pan. Add the quinoa and stir until fragrant, about 2 minutes. Remove the pan from the heat and add 1½ cups cool water then stir, cover, and return the pan to low heat. Bring the quinoa to a simmer and cook until the liquid is fully absorbed, about 15 minutes.

4 In a medium bowl stir together the carrots and cooked quinoa and season well with salt and pepper then reserve.

SAUCE

1 Heat a medium soup pot over high heat. Add the olive oil and wait for it to shimmer then add the onion and cook for 8 minutes or until pale brown. Add the garlic and cook for 1 minute more.

2 Add the water, and chopped tomatoes and all their juices from the pan. Stir in all the seasonings and reduce the heat to low. Simmer for approximately 8 minutes then remove the sauce from the heat. Season the sauce with salt and pepper and reserve until assembly.

TOPPING

1 In a small saucepan bring the cashews to a boil in 2 cups of water. Remove the pot from the heat and allow the cashews to soak for about 30 minutes then drain the liquid. Using a blender: puree the almond milk and cashews until smooth and set it aside.

2 Cut the tofu into four equal slabs and squeeze it in a paper towel–lined kitchen towel until it bursts. Push the tofu through a potato ricer or whisk it in a medium bowl until it is completely smooth then set the tofu aside.

3 Melt the butter in a small saucepan and stir in the flour, nutmeg, salt, and pepper with a wooden spoon. Whisk in the cashew mixture and bring it to a gentle simmer. Simmer the sauce until it is considerably thick, about 15 minutes, then mix in the yeast. Remove the pan from the heat and season the sauce to taste with salt and pepper. Reserve the topping until assembly.

ASSEMBLY

1 Preheat the oven to 350°F. Lightly oil the bottom and sides of a 9 x 11-inch casserole dish or something similar.

2 Line the bottom of the dish with slices of grilled eggplant. Drizzle a small amount of sauce over the eggplant. Top the eggplant with the quinoa-carrot mixture. Distribute all the tomato sauce over the quinoa and top the quinoa with the remaining slices of eggplant. Spoon the topping over the eggplant slices and completely cover the surface.

3 Bake the moussaka 35 to 40 minutes, or until golden brown on top. Let the moussaka cool for 10 to 15 minutes before slicing

LEFTOVER MOUSSAKA IS GOOD FOR 4 DAYS REFRIGERATED OR 2 MONTHS FROZEN. AS WITH OTHER DISHES, I RECOMMEND FREEZING THIS IN PORTIONS SO THAT YOU CAN DEFROST AS LITTLE AS NEEDED.

NOTE:

If you really want to make this in individual servings you can use big ramekins or oval au gratin dishes. Just be sure to rotate them after about 20 minutes to achieve even browning.

MUSHROOM, SPINACH, *and* RICOTTA-STUFFED ENCHILADAS

MAKES 5 SERVINGS

One of the best things about enchiladas is how durable they are. They can be made up to 2 days ahead of time and refrigerated, then all you have to do is just pop them in the oven and serve. (Leftover enchiladas are great, too; I admit to eating them cold sometimes.) Corn tortillas make this dish completely gluten-free but they are not as durable as small flour tortillas; whatever you decide to use, the end product will be delicious.

1 batch Almond-Tofu Ricotta (page 11)

1 batch Quick and Easy Enchilada Sauce (page 206)

2 tablespoons extra-virgin olive oil

1 pound button mushrooms, sliced thin

Kosher salt and freshly ground black pepper to taste

1 pound fresh baby spinach

10 corn tortillas or taco-size flour tortillas

1 cup grated vegan cheddar cheese (optional)

1 small red onion, minced

2 tablespoons dried oregano

1 Prepare the ricotta and enchilada sauce first.

2 Heat a large skillet or sauté pan over high heat and add the olive oil then wait for it to shimmer, about 20 seconds. Add the mushrooms and cook, stirring often until they are wilted and brown (about 10 minutes). Season the mushrooms with salt and pepper then continue cooking and stirring until the pan appears dry. Remove the pan from the heat and place the mushrooms in a small bowl and set them aside to cool.

3 Mound the fresh spinach in a large skillet and place the skillet over medium heat. It should only take a minute or 2 for the spinach to start wilting. Turn and stir the spinach until it has completely wilted and liquid is visible in the pan. Remove the pan from the heat and allow the spinach to cool. Line a strong kitchen towel with a paper towel and place the wilted spinach in the center. Bring the corners of the towel together to form a pouch and squeeze as much liquid out of the spinach as possible. (Twist the towel tight and really put some muscle into it!) Roughly chop the spinach and fluff it with your fingers then fold the spinach and sautéed mushrooms into the Almond-Tofu Ricotta.

4 In a hot dry skillet or over an open flame, cook the tortillas for 20 to 30 seconds per side. As you cook the tortillas stack them on top of each other to steam and soften them further.

ASSEMBLY

1 Preheat the oven to 350°F.

2 Use an 8 x 12-inch casserole dish or something similar. Pour just enough enchilada sauce to cover the bottom of the casserole dish. Fill each tortilla with about ½ cup of the ricotta mixture and roll the tortilla up. Place the enchiladas in the casserole dish side-by-side until all 10 tortillas have been filled.

3 Ladle enchilada sauce over each enchilada until they are all covered in sauce. Distribute the vegan cheese (if using) evenly over the enchiladas.

4 Bake the enchiladas uncovered for 20 to 25 minutes. While the enchiladas are baking mix the red onion with dried oregano in a small bowl.

5 Remove the enchiladas from the oven and distribute the diced onion mixture evenly over the enchiladas. Serve hot.

ENCHILADAS ARE GOOD FOR 3 TO 4 DAYS REFRIGERATED OR UP TO TWO MONTHS FROZEN.

NOTE:

Enchiladas are commonly served with refried beans and rice. Personally, I find that combo a bit too heavy. Try serving these airy 'chiladas with a light soup like my Roasted Red Bell Pepper Soup (page 96) or with a bright, crisp salad like the Shaved Fennel with Arugula Crunch Salad (page 135).

quick and easy enchilada sauce

MAKES 3½ CUPS

This is super easy and way better than those watery canned enchilada sauces.

2 tablespoons extra-virgin olive oil

1 medium white onion, chopped

4 garlic cloves, crushed

Two 14.5-oz cans diced tomatoes, drained

2 tablespoons chili powder

1 tablespoon cumin

2 tablespoons dried oregano

1 teaspoon kosher salt

1 Heat a medium saucepan over high heat and add the olive oil. When the oil is hot add the onion and stir until slightly brown, about 5 minutes. Add the garlic and stir for an additional 2 minutes then remove the pan from the heat.

2 Place the onion mixture in a blender with the tomatoes and puree the mixture until smooth. (Add a small amount of water if necessary to get the mixture going.)

3 Return the pureed tomato sauce to the saucepan and bring the sauce to a gentle simmer over medium-low heat. When the sauce comes to a simmer, stir in the chili powder, cumin, oregano, and salt. Let the sauce simmer gently for about 10 minutes. Remove the pan from the heat and allow it to cool.

SAUCE IS GOOD FOR 1 WEEK REFRIGERATED OR 3 MONTHS FROZEN.

JACKFRUIT SOFT TACOS
in GUAJILLO SAUCE

MAKES 6 SERVINGS

If you've never had jackfruit, my friend, you are in for a treat. Most of us will have to settle for the canned versions, which are available online and in most Asian markets (but if you can get your hands on some fresh jackfruit then go ahead and rock-out with that giant gummy monster). There are usually two types of canned available: in brine and in syrup. I use the syrup version in this recipe because the sweetness balances the spice from the guajillo chile. The star here is the guajillo sauce. It is not too spicy but rich and full flavored; once you make this sauce and see how easy it is the sky's the limit. It makes a terrific enchilada sauce and it's good poured over rice or mixed into a tofu scramble. Or, you know, just eat it with a spoon.

3 cans jackfruit, in syrup

8 guajillo chiles, stemmed and seeded

2 tablespoons safflower or grapeseed oil

1 small white onion, chopped

6 garlic cloves, chopped

10 firm Roma tomatoes, peeled using easy-peel method (page 40)

1 tablespoon tomato paste

1 teaspoon dried oregano

1 teaspoon cumin

1 teaspoon kosher salt

1 cup Better than Bouillon "No Chicken" Chicken Broth or Rich Yellow Vegetable Stock (page 116)

ACCOMPANIMENTS:

2 cups shredded green cabbage

1 firm avocado, cut into wedges

Corn or flour tortillas

NOTES:

If you can't find jackfruit and you don't want to wait for it to be delivered to your house by a drone, I recommend using a firm, meaty vegetable like grated celeriac, chopped cauliflower, or any type of Gardein product.

The recipe can be made with different dried chiles like pasilla or chiles negros, but guajillos are the best in my opinion.

(CONTINUED) >

> (CONTINUED FROM PREVIOUS PAGE)

1 Drain, rinse, and squeeze the jackfruit dry with paper towels. Shred the fruit with your fingers, then place the fruit in a bowl and set it aside.

2 Rub the dry chiles clean with a wet paper towel and let them air dry. Using a pair of scissors cut the tops off the chiles and slice them open to remove the seeds and rib membrane.

3 Heat a large dry cast-iron pan or skillet over medium heat then add the oil. Soften the dried chiles in the warm oil, turning them often to cook all sides until they are slightly puffed and fragrant, about 2 minutes. Remove the chiles from the pan and let them cool.

4 Turn the heat to high and add the onions and cook until they are light brown, about 10 minutes. Add the garlic and cook about 1 to 2 minutes more then add the tomatoes, tomato paste, chiles, oregano, cumin, and salt. Stir the sauce with a wooden spoon until the juices begin to simmer and reduce about 5 minutes only. Remove the pan from the heat and let the sauce cool slightly. Carefully place the sauce in the blender with the broth and puree until smooth.

5 Combine the shredded jackfruit with the guajillo sauce in a soup pot and bring to a gentle simmer. Serve the jackfruit with corn or flour tortillas, shredded cabbage, and avocado wedges.

THE JACKFRUIT AND SAUCE ARE GOOD FOR 4 DAYS IN THE FRIDGE AND 3 MONTHS IN THE FREEZER.

TIP:

When blending hot liquids always use the lid but remove the little fill cap and cover the hole with a folded kitchen towel. The idea is to allow air to escape from the pitcher and prevent the hot liquid from jumping out of the pitcher and causing harm. ("The more you know . . .")

8 | IF ALL GOOD MEALS MUST COME TO AN END ...
(let's go out this way)

AMARETTI COOKIES

MAKES ABOUT 40 COOKIES

These cookies are traditionally dependent on fluffy egg whites for their shape and texture. Well, tofu to the rescue. These puppies are crisp and crunchy on the outside, soft on the inside, and completely addictive.

8 ounces Homemade Almond Paste (page 213)

1 cup powdered sugar

2 ounces silken tofu

1 teaspoon almond extract

1 tablespoon + 1 teaspoon baking powder

¾ cup flaxseed meal

1 cup all-purpose flour

Extra powdered sugar for dusting cookies

1 Prepare the almond paste first and allow it to cool.

2 Preheat the oven to 350°F. Line two baking sheets with parchment paper.

3 Place the almond paste in a food processor with the sugar. Pulse until the mixture is well combined. Add the tofu and almond extract then pulse until the dough is well combined.

4 In a medium bowl, mix the baking powder, flaxseed meal, and flour. Pulse this flour mixture in three stages into the almond paste mixture then continue processing the dough until it is very smooth.

5 Fill a pastry bag with the almond dough and twist the top closed. Lay the tip of the bag flat and cut the bag at ½ inch across the tip. Pipe 1½-inch mounds onto the parchment paper, spaced about 1 inch apart. Using a wet fingertip or a damp paper towel, lightly press the top of each cookie to remove any peaks left behind from the piping process. Lightly sprinkle a little sugar on top of each cookie.

6 Bake the cookies immediately for 15 to 20 minutes or until the cookies are a deep golden brown. Remove the cookies from the oven and allow them to cool completely before gently peeling the cookies from the parchment paper. Dust the cookies with additional powdered sugar if you like. Serve the amaretti cookies immediately or store the cookies in an airtight container.

COOKIES ARE GOOD FOR 2 WEEKS AT ROOM TEMPERATURE; 4 MONTHS IN THE FREEZER. TO DEFROST, PLACE THE COOKIES ON A PLATE AND LET THEM DEFROST ON THE COUNTER.

NOTE:

This recipe calls for a pastry bag but if you don't have one you can always use a gallon-size resealable plastic bag and push the filling toward one corner of the bag then continue with the instructions.

homemade almond paste

MAKES 12 OUNCES (1½ CUPS)

½ cup organic white sugar

2 tablespoons maple syrup

⅓ cup water

1½ cups almond flour

1 Place the sugar, maple syrup, and water in a small saucepan over medium heat. Maintain a gentle simmer until the sugar is dissolved, about 3 minutes.

2 Place the almond flour in the food processor. Remove the simmering sugar from the heat and carefully pour it into the almond flour. Blend the mixture until smooth.

3 Wrap the almond paste in plastic wrap and allow it to cool.

STICKY DATE MUFFINS

MAKES 24 SMALL MUFFINS

These little guys are so easy to make and so delicious it's ridiculous. The sauce tastes like it is complicated to make but it is a snap and it takes the muffins to the next level. Make a platter of these and bring them to a party—they will disappear fast!

1½ pounds dates, pitted and chopped

½ cup hot water

⅓ cup flaxseed meal

8 ounces (1 cup) vegan butter, softened, plus more for greasing muffin tins

½ cup organic brown sugar

2 teaspoons vanilla extract

1¾ cups all-purpose flour

3 tablespoons baking powder

1 teaspoon baking soda

1 teaspoon salt

1 batch Butterscotch Sauce (page 237)

1 Preheat the oven to 350°F. Butter 2 dozen small muffin tins.

2 Place the dates in a medium saucepan with 3 cups of water. Over high heat, bring the dates to a boil and stir. Simmer the dates for 8 minutes then remove them from the heat and allow them to cool. Reserve 1 cup of the liquid from the dates and discard the rest. Place the dates and 1 cup of liquid in a food processor and pulse until smooth. Set the cooked date mixture aside.

3 In a small bowl mix the ½ cup of hot water and flaxseed meal until combined; set the mixture aside to cool.

4 Cream the butter, sugar, and vanilla extract together in a stand mixer or by hand until light and creamy. Add the flax mixture and whip it until it is well incorporated.

5 In a separate bowl combine the flour, baking powder, baking soda, and salt. Add the dry ingredients into the butter, sugar, and flax mixture and give it a stir to combine. Add the pureed date mixture in thirds, being careful to scrape down the sides of the bowl in between batches until the batter is well combined.

6 Fill each muffin cup to just below the rim. Bake for about 20 minutes (depending on the muffin size) or until a toothpick comes out clean. While the muffins are baking make the butterscotch sauce.

ASSEMBLY

1 Remove the cooled muffins from the tin. Place the sticky muffins upside down and poke the bottoms all over with a toothpick to allow the sauce to penetrate.

2 Just before serving reheat the muffins upside down in a 350°F oven or in a warm toaster oven. When the muffins are warm pour a bit of the sauce over the top, about 2 tablespoons each, and serve immediately.

THE MUFFINS WILL KEEP FOR OVER 1 WEEK IN THE FRIDGE. THEY FREEZE WELL, TOO, BUT I RECOMMEND FREEZING THE RAW BATTER INSTEAD, THEN BAKING THEM FRESH WHEN NEEDED. MUFFINS AND BATTER ARE GOOD FOR 3 MONTHS FROZEN.

RUSTIC APPLE PIE

MAKES 10 SERVINGS

This pie is easy and fun to make. There are no mistakes here . . . no imperfections . . . every fold is as deliberate as it should be.

6 large Granny Smith apples, peeled, cored, and cut lengthwise into quarters

½ cup organic brown sugar

3 teaspoons cornstarch

1 teaspoon cinnamon

2 ounces (¼ cup) vegan butter

1 batch Perfect Pie Dough (page 233) or vegan store-bought crust, defrosted and both crusts smashed together.

1 Place the apples in a large bowl and toss them with sugar, being careful to separate all the apple pieces that stick together. Sprinkle 1 teaspoon of cornstarch in the apples and toss. Do this two more times to prevent the cornstarch from clumping when cooked. Sprinkle the cinnamon into the apples half a teaspoon at a time in the same fashion.

2 Heat two large skillets over low heat and add 1 ounce of butter to each pan. When the butter is melted add an equal amount of apple to each pan, using a rubber spatula to make sure you get every bit of the liquid that remains in the bowl. Stirring/tossing often, cook the apples over medium heat for about 18 minutes or until the apples are semi-soft and gooey and some pieces show a bit of color.

3 Remove the pans from the heat and combine the apples into one pan, again using a rubber spatula to get all the gooey goodness that remains in the pan. Set the apples aside to cool.

4 Dust a surface generously with flour and roll the piecrust into a 16 to 17–inch circle. (You might find this easier rolling the crust in between two large sheets of parchment paper.)

ASSEMBLY

1 Carefully place the rolled piecrust on the center of a sheet tray. Dump the apples in the center of the large piecrust. Arrange the apples in the very center in a nice circular fashion, leaving the rest of the apples at random. Fold one edge over the top of the pie and continue folding the edges up and over. *Note: don't stress, this is a rustic pie—there is no wrong way to do this.* Refrigerate the unbaked pie for 20 minutes to firm up the crust.

2 Preheat the oven to 400°F.

3 Bake the pie for 20 minutes or until the crust is crisp and golden brown. Serve warm.

PIE IS GOOD FOR 3 TO 4 DAYS LEFT OUT AND UP TO 1 WEEK IN THE FRIDGE.

APPLE DATE PECAN BARS

MAKES 8 SERVINGS

Don't let the lengthy instructions scare you . . . this is one of the easiest desserts to put together. I find that too often desserts are too filling or so sweet that you can't taste the nuances of the ingredients. That's not the case here. This is the perfect type of treat when you want something to satisfy your sweet tooth but not induce a coma. Serve it after dinner but save some for the next day to have with your afternoon tea or coffee.

FOR THE CRUST

4 ounces coconut oil or 4 ounces (½ cup) vegan butter

1¼ cups all-purpose flour

1 cup masa harina or corn flour

½ teaspoon kosher salt

2 tablespoons coconut sugar or organic brown sugar

⅓ cup ice water, plus more if necessary

FOR THE FILLING

1½ cups (12 ounces) dates, pitted

½ cup uncooked oats

FOR THE TOPPING

4 ounces (½ cup) vegan butter, melted

⅓ cup silken tofu

¼ cup coconut sugar or organic brown sugar

6 ounces pecan pieces, plus whole pecan halves to decorate

2 large Granny Smith apples

CRUST

1 Place small dollops of the coconut oil onto a plate and freeze (or, if using butter, cut it into small cubes and freeze).

2 Place the flours, salt, and sugar in the bowl of a food processor and pulse to combine. Add the butter or solid coconut oil and pulse a few times more. Pour in the ice water and pulse again until mixture is crumbly and will stick together when you squeeze it. Add more ice water a tablespoon at a time if necessary.

3 Place the dough onto a dry surface and shape it into a fat disk. Wrap it in plastic wrap or place it in a in a freezer bag and refrigerate the dough for 30 minutes minimum and up to 2 days.

(CONTINUED) >

NOTES:

The masa harina (a corn flour used to make tortillas) is the key ingredient in the crust. It gives the tart a distinct earthy flavor that works perfectly with the sweetness of the dates.

The components here are pretty versatile, too. The chopped apple topping resembles charoset (the traditional Passover dish and my favorite) and the date filling can be made on its own and used as a spreadable jam.

A 10-inch fluted tart pan works best here but any pie pan will do the job.

> (CONTINUED FROM PREVIOUS PAGE)

4 After the dough has rested, unwrap it and place it onto a clean, dry surface that has been dusted lightly with flour and roll the crust out big and thin. Press the dough gingerly into a 10-inch fluted tart pan or pie pan and allow the sides to come up about ¼ inch above the edge of the pan then cut the excess dough with a knife or scissors. Refrigerate the crust again for 20 minutes to prevent shrinkage.

5 Preheat the oven to 375°F.

6 Pierce the crust all over with the tines of a fork. Cover it with a large piece of parchment paper and fill it with pie weights or dry beans or rice. Bake the crust for 15 minutes. Carefully remove the weights by picking up the parchment paper by the corners. If using beans or rice save them in a container to use again for the same purpose.

FILLING

1 Bring 2 cups of water to a rolling boil. Remove water from the heat, add the seeded dates and stir. Allow the dates to steep for 10 minutes. Strain the dates and allow them to cool.

2 Place the dates in the food processor and pulse until smooth. Add the oats and pulse until well combined. Place the filling in a plastic bag and set aside. Don't bother washing the food processor yet, you'll need it for the apple topping.

TOPPING

1 In a medium bowl combine the melted butter, tofu, and sugar.

2 Place the pecans in the food processor and pulse for a few seconds until they are chopped. Add the chopped pecans to the tofu mixture.

3 Peel, core, and quarter the apples. Cut each quarter in half. Pulse the apples in a food processor until they are finely chopped, about 12 seconds. Place the chopped apples on paper towels or a clean kitchen towel and squeeze them firmly over the sink to remove excess moisture. Add the apples to the tofu mixture and combine.

ASSEMBLY

1 Preheat the oven to 350°F.

2 Using an offset spatula, spread about a ⅓-inch-thick layer of the date filling over the crust. Evenly distribute the apple topping and bake the tart for 15 to 20 minutes or until the apples are cooked and soft. Serve at warm, to room, temperature.

THE TART IS PRESERVED BEST WHEN COVERED AND LEFT AT ROOM TEMPERATURE BUT IT IS ONLY GOOD FOR A DAY OR TWO. IT CAN LAST A WEEK IF IT IS COVERED AND REFRIGERATED THE DAY IT IS MADE, BUT IT LOSES SOME OF ITS CRISPNESS.

SUMMER PEACH *and* GINGER CRISP

MAKES 6 SERVINGS

This is not your average peach cobbler, no siree, Bob! This stuff is dangerously addictive. The key ingredient here is ginger; it adds a sharp brightness that cuts the sugar flavor without overpowering the beauty of the peaches. If you find yourself in a pinch, good-quality frozen peaches are better than poor-quality fresh ones.

FOR THE CRUMB TOPPING

2 ounces (¼ cup) vegan butter, cubed and chilled

½ cup quick-cooking oats

¼ cup all-purpose flour

½ cup brown sugar

1 tablespoon cinnamon

¼ cup raw chopped pecans

¼ cup raw sliced almonds

FOR THE FILLING

½ cup coconut sugar or brown sugar

One 1-inch piece fresh ginger, peeled and minced

1 tablespoon cornstarch

2½ pounds firm fresh peaches, peeled, pitted, and cut into ½-inch pieces

1 Mix all the topping ingredients in a medium bowl until crumbly, then refrigerate the mixture until needed.

2 Preheat the oven to 375°F. Butter an 9 x 9-inch or similar casserole dish.

3 Pulse the sugar, ginger, and cornstarch in a food processor until the ginger is finely chopped.

4 In a large bowl toss the peaches with sugar mixture until well combined. Sprinkle the crumb topping evenly over the peaches until well covered. Bake the crisp for about 40 minutes or until bubbling and brown.

5 Allow the crisp to cool at least 15 minutes before serving.

LEFTOVER PEACH CRISP IS GOOD FOR 4 DAYS IN THE FRIDGE AND 2 DAYS LEFT OUT AT ROOM TEMPERATURE. REFRIGERATION WILL PROLONG THE LIFE OF THE COBBLER BUT IT WILL ALSO MAKE THE TOPPING SOGGY. I DO NOT RECOMMEND FREEZING.

GLUTEN-FREE APPLE TARTE TATIN

Few desserts are as enamoring and sexy as a well-executed apple tarte tatin. It is perfect in its simplicity. Traditionally it is served on puff pastry or pie crust, but my gluten-free almond flour dough is a perfect crisp companion to the rich moisture of the caramel.

FOR THE CRUST

1 cup almond flour

1 tablespoon organic sugar

4 ounces (½ cup) vegan butter, cut into large cubes and held in the freezer

4+ tablespoons ice water

FOR THE FILLING

8 to 10 medium Granny Smith apples (choose firm ones) or 6 to 8 big Granny Smith apples

4 ounces (½ cup) vegan butter

1 cup organic sugar

CRUST

1 Pulse the flour and sugar in a food processor. Add the frozen butter and pulse just a few times until the butter is chopped into pea-size pieces.

2 Measure the ice water into a small cup. While pulsing add the water to the food processor in a slow, steady stream. The mixture should resemble coarse meal. Pinch the mixture; it should come together easily and be smooth. If it is too dry and crumbly add a dash more ice water and pulse a few times.

3 Dump the mixture out onto a well-floured surface and squeeze it into a dough. Working quickly, roll the dough out into a 10-inch circle. Be sure the crust is just big enough to cover your 8 to 10–inch sauté pan. Cut off any excess dough and slide the crust onto parchment paper or a large plate then put the crust in the refrigerator. This can be done up to 2 days in advance.

FILLING

1 Preheat the oven to 375°F

2 Peel, core, and cut the apples in half. If they are really big, cut them in thirds or quarters.

3 Melt the butter over low heat in an 8 to 10–inch oven-safe sauté pan then remove the pan from the heat. Pour in the sugar and distribute it evenly throughout the pan.

4 Arrange the apples cut side down all around the pan then place as many apple pieces as possible in the center. Custom cut any leftover apple pieces to wedge in during the cooking process. Return the pan to the burner and cook over high heat for 12 minutes or until the liquid in the pan turns a beautiful amber color. Remove the pan from the heat and using metal tongs or a fork, gently turn the apple pieces over. Return the pan to the burner over high heat for 6 minutes and then remove the pan once again from heat.

5 Carefully place the crust on top of the apples and brush off any excess flour. Tuck the edges in slightly along the inside of the pan. Bake the tart in the oven until the crust is dry and firm, about 25 minutes.

6 Remove the tart from the oven and allow it to cool about 20 minutes. Run a sharp knife along the inside edge of the pan. Place a round dish on top of the pan. Take a deep breath. With one hand over the dish and the other holding the pan, flip the pan over onto the dish in one smooth motion. Cut the tart with a sharp knife and serve warm.

THE TARTE TATIN CAN BE COVERED AND LEFT OUT FOR 1 TO 2 DAYS BEFORE IT NEEDS TO BE REFRIGERATED. THE TART DOES NOT FREEZE WELL.

> **NOTE:**
>
> For best results be sure you are using a true sauté pan, which has straight (45°) sides. A pan with rounded sides is a skillet and it will work, but it is not ideal.

SILKY CHOCOLATE MOUSSE

MAKES 8 SERVINGS

Vegan chocolate mousse is pretty common but some are frankly . . . gross. Snorting a line of cocoa powder sounds more enjoyable than some of these recipes I've seen. I'd rather have a tablespoon of something really good than a gallon of some goofy "healthy" version of the same thing.

With that being said this recipe is decadent but still *way* better for you than its artificial, animal fat–based counterparts and a little goes a long way. The whipped cream is a decadent bonus but not necessary.

---

1 block silken tofu, liquid drained

¾ cup organic white sugar

1 cup raw blanched cashews, soaked overnight and drained, or simmered for 5 minutes then soaked for 1 hour and drained

12 ounces semisweet baking chocolate, or good-quality chocolate chips (I like Ghirardelli)

4 ounces (½ cup) vegan butter

Super-Easy Coconut Whipped Cream (optional, page 234)

1 In a food processor puree the tofu and sugar until smooth then place the tofu in a medium bowl. (No need to clean the bowl yet.)

2 Place the soaked cashews and 1 cup water in the food processor and puree until smooth, periodically scraping down the sides of the bowl. Using a rubber spatula, press the cashew puree through a fine-mesh strainer into the tofu mixture to remove any un-pureed nuts.

3 Melt the chocolate and butter in a metal bowl over simmering water or in the microwave in a glass bowl in 30-second intervals. Stir the chocolate with a rubber spatula to ensure it is melted and smooth. Incorporate the chocolate into the tofu mixture until smooth then cover and chill at least 30 minutes.

4 When it's firm and cold, whip the mixture with a hand mixer until it achieves a mousse-like texture. Serve in ramekins, martini glasses, whatever your heart desires. Garnish with whipped cream (if using) and chocolate shavings just before serving.

MOUSSE IS GOOD FOR 1 WEEK REFRIGERATED.

KAISERSCHMARRN

MAKES 4 SERVINGS

I learned to make Kaiserschmarrn in culinary school from a gnarly Austrian chef. At that time, the Culinary Institute of America had a German president, and he filled the staff with these old tough Austrian and German chefs with thick accents. Fast forward a year later: I found myself cooking for the most famous Austrian-born body-builder/actor/politician ever—so of course I whipped up some Kaiserschmarrn. He flipped out. He was really surprised that this Mexi-Cali chef knew about the 'schmarrn. My wife was also blown away with my practice batches at home and this fluffy shredded pancake has become a classic decadent treat for our family—for dessert or breakfast.

Enjoy this vegan version any time of the day and serve it with your best Austrian-body-builder accent.

2 cups all-purpose flour

½ teaspoon cinnamon

1 tablespoon baking powder

2 tablespoons brown sugar

¼ cup flaxseed meal

1 cup warm water

1 ounce dark rum (optional)

1 cup almond milk

1 teaspoon vanilla extract

2 tablespoons (⅛ cup) melted vegan butter, plus ¼ cup for the pan

1 cup diced fruit

1 In a large bowl combine the flour, cinnamon, baking powder, and sugar.

2 In a medium bowl whisk the flaxseed meal and warm water until well combined. Whisk the rum (if using), almond milk, vanilla extract, and butter into the flaxseed meal mixture. Mix the wet ingredients into the dry and whisk until smooth.

3 Heat a large skillet/frying pan over medium heat and add about 1 tablespoon of vegan butter.

4 Cook the batter like pancakes: Pour ⅓ cup of batter into the pan (you can make two pancakes at a time). Cook for 2 to 3 minutes on one side. When bubbles appear all around the edge of the pancake and the bottom looks golden brown, flip to the other side. Once cooked set the pancakes aside.

5 Add an extra tablespoon of vegan butter to the pan and cook the second batch.

6 Using two forks or your fingers tear the pancakes apart into rough pieces. Add 2 tablespoons of vegan butter to the pan and sauté the fresh fruit until tender then add the torn pancakes and toss to incorporate. Cook, stirring occasionally, for 3 to 5 minutes or until the pancake pieces are golden. The mixture will look like a pile of "unidentifiable stuff," which is the definition of *Schmarrn!*

7 Transfer the Kaiserschmarrn to a serving platter, dust with powdered sugar, and serve.

THIS IS BEST WHEN EATEN RIGHT AWAY.

NOTE:

I like it best with peaches, but you can use whatever you like: apple, plum, nectarine, bananas, fresh cherries . . .

CARROT CAKE *with* WHITE CAKE FROSTING

MAKES 12 SERVINGS

This carrot cake is unbelievably moist and a great crowd pleaser. It also makes great muffins of any size. Chia seeds are awesome for our digestion, so don't hate me because you had to buy a whole bag just to use ¼ cup. Place a spoonful of seeds in your drinking water and sprinkle some in your cereal and salads. If you don't find them at your local market, any health food store will carry them.

Vegan butter, as needed for greasing pans

¼ cup chia seeds

½ block silken tofu

½ cup organic white sugar

1½ cups organic brown sugar

1½ cups grapeseed or safflower oil

2 cups all-purpose flour

1 tablespoon baking powder

1 teaspoon salt

3 teaspoons cinnamon

3 cups grated carrots

1 cup chopped pecans

½ cup toasted and chopped almond slices

1 batch White Cake Frosting (page 230)

1 Preheat oven to 325°F. Prepare two 9-inch round cake pans by rubbing the sides with vegan butter and lining the bottom with parchment paper.

2 Soak chia seeds in ¾ cup warm water for 15 minutes to form a gel. In a large bowl whip the chia gel, tofu, sugars, and oil until well incorporated.

3 In a separate bowl mix the flour, baking powder, salt, and cinnamon. Add the wet ingredients into the dry ingredients and stir until well incorporated. Gently fold in the carrots, pecans, and raisins.

4 Pour batter into the prepared pans. Bake the cakes for 20 minutes then give each cake a 180-degree turn and switch their positions in the oven. Bake the cakes an additional 15 minutes or until a toothpick comes out clean.

5 When the cakes are done leave them in the pan and let them cool at least 2 hours or overnight. I like to refrigerate the cakes so they are firm when I frost them, but it is not necessary.

(CONTINUED) >

> **NOTE:**
>
> If you are using a smaller than 9-inch cake pan, your cake will take longer to bake. If you are using a larger than 9-inch cake pan, your cake will bake faster.

FROSTING

1 Place the first cake layer on a cake stand or large plate right side up. Note: If the cake is profoundly bulbous gently cut it flat by trimming the top with a serrated knife then do the same with the other layer.

2 Spread a thin layer of frosting on top of the cake then place the second layer upside down onto the first layer.

3 Frost the cake entirely. Take a good look at your remaining frosting, you have to make this cover the entire cake, so don't go hog wild or your cake will have bald spots.

4 Once the cake is frosted sprinkle the outside with toasted almonds then place it in the fridge to firm up before slicing.

THE CAKE IS GOOD FOR 1 WEEK REFRIGERATED OR 2 MONTHS FROZEN. I RECOMMEND SLICING THE CAKE BEFORE FREEZING IT SO YOU CAN DEFROST ONLY WHAT YOU NEED.

white cake frosting

MAKES 2 CUPS

This is a basic vegan white frosting. It's perfect for the Carrot Cake (page 228) but it is also very versatile. It can be used on cupcakes or add 1 cup melted chocolate chips and you have a terrific chocolate frosting.

½ block silken tofu

1 teaspoon vanilla extract

8 ounces (1 cup) vegan butter, softened

1 pound powdered sugar

1 In a medium bowl whip the tofu, vanilla extract, and butter until well blended. Add the powdered sugar and blend until fully incorporated.

2 Refrigerate the frosting for at least 45 minutes before assembling the cake.

FROSTING IS GOOD FOR 2 WEEKS REFRIGERATED.

WHAT THE FUDGE?

MAKES 6 TO 12 SERVINGS, DEPENDING ON HOW MUCH FUDGE THEY EAT

It doesn't get faster or easier than this. I don't think this even counts as cooking or baking so if you think of yourself as useless in the kitchen, this recipe is for you.

When it comes to purchasing your ingredients there are a few choices to make. I prefer using coconut oil here, but it requires the fudge to stay cool. It doesn't have to live in the refrigerator but I wouldn't bring it to the beach or ship it across the country. Good-quality bittersweet chocolate is more available than ever. Trader Joes has the best price and clear labels, but if you are in a pinch, you can use semisweet chocolate chips, too.

Maldon-brand sea salt is a big-flaked salt that doesn't dissolve easily so it is perfect for when you want that burst of salt to accompany sweetness. Sea salt works fine here, too, because the salt goes on top so it won't dissolve right away.

---

4 ounces coconut oil or 4 ounces (½ cup) vegan butter, plus more for greasing dish

9 ounces bittersweet chocolate (60 to 70% cacao; read labels—lots of vegan options here)

1 cup cocoa powder

½ cup maple syrup

¼ cup sugar

½ cup pistachios, whole

½ cup pecan pieces, toasted

1 teaspoon Maldon sea salt

1 Grease an 8-inch-square glass baking dish or similar with vegan butter or coconut oil and set it aside.

2 Melt the butter and chocolate in a metal bowl over simmering water or in the microwave in a glass bowl in 30-second intervals. Gently whisk in the cocoa, maple syrup, sugar, and nuts and mix until everything is well incorporated.

3 Spread the fudge into the greased dish and refrigerate for 2 hours or until firm. Evenly sprinkle the top of the fudge with the salt and cut the fudge into squares.

FUDGE LASTS FOREVER, RIGHT? AT LEAST 3 WEEKS COVERED AND COOL AND 2 MONTHS FROZEN OR REFRIGERATED.

PERFECT PIE DOUGH

MAKES TWO 9-INCH PIE CRUSTS OR ONE LARGE CRUST FOR A FREE-FORM PIE OR STREUSEL

6 ounces (¾ cup) vegan butter or 6 ounces coconut oil

3⅓ cups all-purpose flour, or whole wheat flour if you prefer

1½ teaspoons salt

2 tablespoons coconut sugar

½ cup ice water, or more if necessary

1 Cut the butter in cubes and freeze (or place small dollops of the coconut oil onto a plate and freeze).

2 Place the flour, salt, and sugar in the bowl of a food processor and pulse to combine. Add the butter or solid coconut oil and pulse a few times. Pour in the ice water and pulse again until mixture is crumbly and will stick together when you squeeze it. Add more ice water a tablespoon at a time if necessary.

3 Dump the dough onto a dry surface and shape it into a fat disk then wrap it in plastic wrap or place it in a in a freezer bag and re-frigerate the dough for 30 minutes minimum and up to 2 days.

THE DOUGH IS GOOD FOR 3 MONTHS FROZEN. FREEZE IN A THIN, FLAT DISK FOR QUICK DEFROSTING.

SUPER-EASY COCONUT WHIPPED CREAM

MAKES 1 CUP

Two 13.5-ounce cans coconut milk

⅓ cup powdered sugar, agave syrup, or maple syrup (use more if desired)

2 teaspoons vanilla extract, vanilla bean paste, or freshly scraped vanilla bean

1 Refrigerate the coconut milk overnight. Chill a mixing bowl.

2 Using a can opener, open the bottom of the canned milk and pour the liquid into a bowl or container. (Save this liquid for smoothies or add it to the cooking liquid when making rice.) Scoop out the firm coconut milk into the chilled mixing bowl.

3 Add the sweetener of choice and vanilla extract then whip the cream with a whisk or hand mixer until light and fluffy. Serve immediately or refrigerate until needed. The cream will stiffen in the fridge but it takes a few hours before you need to rewhip it.

CREAM IS GOOD FOR 2 WEEKS REFRIGERATED.

WHIPPED CREAM *(No Coconut)*

MAKES A BIT MORE THAN 1 CUP

Coconut milk–based whipped cream is delicious, but some people don't like coconut and sometimes that flavor just doesn't belong, and for those instances, there is this recipe.

Don't get sketched out by the use of xanthan gum in this recipe: it's a stabilizer/thickener like cornstarch, except cornstarch needs to be heated to work and xanthan gum does not. Yes, there is a half cup of oil used here, but let's remember we are making whipped cream, not a smoothie. Besides, those 10 calorie, 0 carb, 0 fat, whipped creams? Do we really know what that stuff is made of?

½ cup ice-cold almond milk

½ cup neutral oil like canola, safflower, or grapeseed

¼ cup powdered sugar, agave syrup, or maple syrup

1 teaspoon vanilla extract, vanilla bean paste, or freshly scraped vanilla bean

⅛ teaspoon xanthan gum

1 Place all ingredients in a high-speed blender or food processor. If using the blender, start on low variable speed and increase to high.

2 Blend until whipped and creamy then chill about 45 minutes or until cold.

CREAM IS GOOD FOR 2 WEEKS REFRIGERATED.

HAZELNUT CHOCOLATE SPREAD

MAKES 3 CUPS

"Nut-hell-yeah"—who doesn't like that commercial stuff? But it's not vegan and it also has some less-than-natural-sounding ingredients. This spread is easy to make and just as yummy and versatile as the commercial brand. Try it with almond butter and bananas.

2½ cups (about 12 ounces) raw hazelnuts

1 cup almond milk

½ teaspoon kosher salt

6 ounces dark chocolate (70% cacao or higher), chopped

1 tablespoon vanilla extract

⅓ cup cocoa powder

¼ cup agave syrup or maple syrup

3 tablespoons coconut oil

1 In a large saucepan bring 8 cups of salted water to a rolling boil. Carefully add the hazelnuts to the water and boil them for 15 minutes. Remove from heat, drain the nuts, and place them on a sheet tray or large plate to cool. When the nuts are cool enough to handle rub them in your palms to remove the skins. Set the peeled nuts aside.

2 In a small saucepan over medium heat bring the almond milk and salt to a simmer, then remove from the heat and stir in the chocolate until it is completely melted. Place the chocolate mixture in a blender and add the hazelnuts, vanilla extract, cocoa powder, agave syrup, and oil. Blend the spread until smooth, stopping periodically to scrape down the sides with a rubber spatula. Use right away or store refrigerated in an airtight container.

SPREAD IS GOOD FOR 2 WEEKS.

BUTTERSCOTCH SAUCE

This sauce is downright drinkable. It elevates the date muffins into something really special but it also could be drizzled over ice cream or vegan bread pudding.

1 cup almond milk

¼ cup raw cashews, brought to a boil in water then soaked for 30 minutes

4 ounces (½ cup) vegan butter

1 cup brown sugar

1 teaspoon vanilla extract

4 ounces dark rum (optional)

1 Drain and rinse the soaked cashews.

2 Using a blender, puree the almond milk and cashews until smooth.

3 Combine the cashew mixture, butter, sugar, vanilla extract, and rum (if using) in a saucepan over medium heat and bring the mixture to a simmer while whisking. Simmer gently for about 10 minutes then remove the sauce from the heat. Let the sauce cool before using. Store any leftover sauce in the fridge in an airtight container.

SAUCE IS GOOD FOR 1 WEEK REFRIGERATED OR 3 MONTHS FROZEN.

METRIC CONVERSIONS

- The recipes in this book have not been tested with metric measurements, so some variations might occur.

- Remember that the weight of dry ingredients varies according to the volume or density factor: 1 cup of flour weighs far less than 1 cup of sugar.

GENERAL FORMULA FOR METRIC CONVERSION

Ounces to grams	ounces × 28.35 = grams
Grams to ounces	grams × 0.035 = ounces
Pounds to grams	pounds × 453.5 = grams
Pounds to kilograms	pounds × 0.45 = kilograms
Cups to liters	cups × 0.24 = liters
Fahrenheit to Celsius	(°F − 32) × 5 ÷ 9 = °C
Celsius to Fahrenheit	(°C × 9) ÷ 5 + 32 = °F

VOLUME (LIQUID) MEASUREMENTS

1 teaspoon = ⅙ fluid ounce = 5 milliliters

1 tablespoon = ½ fluid ounce = 15 milliliters

2 tablespoons = 1 fluid ounce = 30 milliliters

¼ cup = 2 fluid ounces = 60 milliliters

⅓ cup = 2⅔ fluid ounces = 79 milliliters

½ cup = 4 fluid ounces = 118 milliliters

1 cup or ½ pint = 8 fluid ounces = 250 milliliters

2 cups or 1 pint = 16 fluid ounces = 500 milliliters

4 cups or 1 quart = 32 fluid ounces = 1,000 milliliters

1 gallon = 4 liters

VOLUME (DRY) MEASUREMENTS

¼ teaspoon = 1 milliliter

½ teaspoon = 2 milliliters

¾ teaspoon = 4 milliliters

1 teaspoon = 5 milliliters

1 tablespoon = 15 milliliters

¼ cup = 59 milliliters

⅓ cup = 79 milliliters

½ cup = 118 milliliters

⅔ cup = 158 milliliters

¾ cup = 177 milliliters

1 cup = 225 milliliters

4 cups or 1 quart = 1 liter

OVEN TEMPERATURE EQUIVALENTS, FAHRENHEIT (F) AND CELSIUS (C)

100°F = 38°C

200°F = 95°C

250°F = 120°C

300°F = 150°C

350°F = 180°C

400°F = 205°C

450°F = 230°C

WEIGHT (MASS) MEASUREMENTS

1 ounce = 30 grams

2 ounces = 55 grams

3 ounces = 85 grams

4 ounces = ¼ pound = 125 grams

8 ounces = ½ pound = 240 grams

12 ounces = ¾ pound = 375 grams

16 ounces = 1 pound = 454 grams

LINEAR MEASUREMENTS

½ inch = 1½ centimeters

1 inch = 2½ centimeters

6 inches = 15 centimeters

8 inches = 20 centimeters

10 inches = 25 centimeters

12 inches = 30 centimeters

20 inches = 50 centimeters

GRACIAS!

Teena, my wife and soulmate, I owe you a huge thank you for all your love, hard work, and patience throughout the book-writing process.

My two awesome boys, Jackson and Trenton, are a constant source of inspiration and drive. I'm sooo grateful to you both for making fatherhood the greatest journey of my life.

Other big thanks go to:

Ellen and Portia, for recognizing my talent and personality and for your continued support and endorsement.

My editor, Renee Sedliar, for your diligence and hours of labor, counsel, and direction. You sculpted a great book out of me, and I'm truly grateful!

The gang at Da Capo (especially John Radziewicz, Kate Burke, Lissa Warren, Kevin Hanover, Claire Ivett, and Jonathan Sainsbury), for your dedication and steadfast efforts to make this book something special. A special shout-out to Christine Marra, Megan Jones, Martha Whitt, Josephine Mariea, and Jean DeBarbieri, for putting it all together and making the book look great.

My fabulous photographer Jannah Eilanie Szeibert—you rock! Your dedication to this book's success has been awesome and inspiring.

Gabriel Gastelum, for getting a great cover photo in the rain.

Reece Williams, for your friendship, creativity, and ever-positive attitude during some pretty long days.

Brian and Jennifer Johnson, for your friendship and the impromptu use of your kitchen!

My wonderful recipe testers and underpaid food stylists, Elaine Vidal-Rahencamp, Katie Belanger, and Sophia Green—you were all terrific!

I owe a very special thanks to the folks at Gardein: Yves Potvin, Russell Barnett, Chef Jason Stefanko, and everyone at the Gardein Test Kitchen in Marina Del Rey for being extremely gracious hosts by allowing me to basically take over for a week and half. I love all of you guys.

Extra-special thank yous go to:

My big, beautiful, and supportive family in Missouri for all your love and encouragement.

My wonderful in-laws, Bill and June Weibking, for all your guidance, friendship, and unconditional love. I'm really fortunate to have a mother- and father in-law I actually look forward to seeing!

Finally, thank you to my massive family, my mom and dad, brothers and sisters, in-laws, and nieces and nephews who continue to inspire, support, and endorse me to everyone they know. I love each and every one of you, and I am eternally grateful to have you all in my life.

INDEX